THE NAKED TOURIST

ALSO BY LAWRENCE OSBORNE

The Accidental Connoisseur

THE
NAKED TOURIST

IN SEARCH OF ADVENTURE AND BEAUTY

IN THE AGE OF THE AIRPORT MALL

LAWRENCE OSBORNE

NORTH POINT PRESS

A DIVISION OF FARRAR, STRAUS AND GIROUX

NEW YORK

North Point Press
A division of Farrar, Straus and Giroux
19 Union Square West, New York 10003

Distributed in Canada by Douglas & McIntyre Ltd.
Printed in the United States of America
First edition, 2006

A section of this book first appeared in *The New Yorker* in slightly different form.

Library of Congress Cataloging-in-Publication Data
Osborne, Lawrence, 1958–
    The naked tourist : in search of adventure and beauty in the
age of the airport mall / Lawrence Osborne.— 1st ed.
        p.   cm.
    ISBN-13: 978-0-86547-709-4 (hardcover : alk. paper)
    ISBN-10: 0-86547-709-4 (hardcover : alk. paper)
    1. Osborne, Lawrence, 1958—Travel.   2. Voyages
and travels.   I. Title.

G465.O82 2006
910.4092—dc22

                                        2005033089

Designed by Jonathan D. Lippincott

www.fsgbooks.com

1   3   5   7   9   10   8   6   4   2

For Tad
many travels

This life is a hospital where every patient is possessed with the desire to change beds; one man would like to suffer in front of the stove, and another believes that he would recover his health beside the window.

It always seems to me that I should feel well in the place where I am not, and this question of removal is one which I discuss incessantly with my soul.

—Charles Baudelaire, "Anywhere Out of the World,"
Le Spleen de Paris

CONTENTS

TRAVELER,
ANTHROPOLOGIST, TOURIST

It came upon me quite suddenly, like a mental disorder unknown to psychiatry: the desire to stop everything in normal life, to uproot and leave. It could be a disease of early middle age, a premature taste of senility: the need to leave the world as it is today behind and find somewhere else. You pack your belongings with a bitter fatalism, as if you know that it is now time to get moving again, to regress to nomadism. You pack your bags, but you have nowhere to go. It is like being dressed up for a ball long after the ballroom has burned down. The desire is there, but there is no object for it.

I leafed through a hundred Web sites—tour group organizations, government brochures, fact sheets, traveler accounts. But the problem of the modern traveler is that he has nowhere left to go. The entire world is a tourist installation, and the awful taste of simulacrum is continually in his mouth. I searched high and low, but nowhere satisfied the need to *leave the world*. I thought for a while of simply checking into a hotel in Hawaii and sitting there for two weeks in front of a television. Somewhere like the Hilton Waikoloa, perhaps, where I could laze on an artificial beach and take a monorail to the hotel nightclub. That would be more interesting than trekking with a small group through Patagonia or winging through the rain forest canopy of Costa Rica in a cable car. I could stay in New York and travel by subway to the forlorn Edgar Allan Poe house in the Bronx. No one goes *there*. There were exotic possibilities, but they were not very exotic—and I wanted something exotic.

Think back to the mood of childhood when you get into the family car and depart for places unknown—how difficult it is to recover the inner dimension of *adventure*. Modern travel is like fast food: short, sharp incursions that do not weave a spell. In our age, tourism has made the planet into a uniform spectacle, and it has made us perpetual strangers wandering through an imitation of an imitation of a place we once wanted to go to. It is the law of diminishing returns.

For a long time I had wanted to take leave of Planet Tourism, to find one of those places that occasionally turn up in the middle pages of newspapers in far-flung cities, in which—we are told—a mad loner has been discovered who has lost all contact with the modern world. It seems inevitable that this desire will one day be listed in the *Diagnostic and Statistical Manual* of the American Psychiatric Association as Robinson Crusoe Syndrome. But the stories are sometimes real. Recall the Japanese soldiers emerging out of Pacific jungles fifty years after their nation's surrender: what stupendous islands, we would like to know, had they been lost on? Once, flying around Indonesia, a journalist from Jakarta I was traveling with pointed down to the bewildering archipelagos of paradise isles below us, somewhere near Molucca, and said that he knew for a fact of a group of Germans who had sailed to one of them in 1967 and had never been seen since. All he knew was that a small local airline dropped them beer every few months. There were so many hundreds of islands that the wandering Teutons had simply disappeared. But I wanted to know *which* island they were on, if they existed at all. Because it's a potent idea, this promise of leaving the world, even if we know it's a myth.

Tourism is the world's largest industry, generating annual revenues of $500 billion. It defines the economies of scores of nations and cities across the globe. Between 1950 and 2002, the number of international travelers, including business travelers, rose from 25 million to 700 million a year: a sea change in the way the world conducts its affairs. The principal occupation of hundreds of millions of humans is now simply entertaining hundreds of millions of other humans. As for the rise of recreational travel, it is rising at all only because, one might presume, we are bored, because we want to have a transforming experience of some kind in a place other than home. We want a new experience—and we want an experience that is commodified, that can be bought for cold cash, but that is safe.

Tourism has also spawned many subsidiary professions. Not just agents, hoteliers, guides, and resort managers but also what are lugubriously known as "travel writers." A technocratic culture loves to precede the noun "writer" with an adjective, thus assuring itself that the said individual is not a charlatan, that is, a loner with a voice, and that he is not—horror of horrors—just a writer. If you publish something only once about a foreign city, you instantly become a *travel writer.* Thus, I have often found myself called a travel writer, whatever that is, and consequently I have been induced occasionally to make a living at it. Sadly, this has led to a long collusion with the forces of global tourism, to long spells of aimless peregrination across entire continents, to 1,034 hotel rooms in 204 nations. Passing one's time in this way is a novel form of dementia. The hotels all look the same, because they are run by the same people; the places all look the same, because they are shaped by the same economic drives. Everywhere resembles everywhere else, and that is the way it has been designed. One day the whole world could easily be a giant interconnected resort called Wherever.

The Marxist theorist Guy Debord once said, "When the Spectacle is everywhere the spectator is nowhere at home." But at the same time, there comes a moment of revolution in the life of the pathetic travel writer, the man who travels to write and who writes to travel, when the world he has spent half a lifetime crisscrossing begins to taste like so much dead paper. He wants to leave and yet he cannot think how to do it. He wants to transcend being the tourist that he really is and become a true traveler again.

In a way, I reached this point quite early on because I have no home and have not had one in decades. A nomad makes for a perfect tourist, but also for a perfectly disillusioned one. The travel writer in me began to decay almost as soon as he was born, but he did confer upon me the will and the means to construct a kind of grand tour for myself as a farewell to "travel writing," in which I no longer have much faith. But how does one rediscover real travel?

The word "travel" itself is surprisingly old. It dates back

to 1375 and originally derived from the French verb *travailler*, "to toil or labor," which in turn derived from the Latin word for a three-pronged stake used as an instrument of torture. Travel began, therefore, with the notion of doing something extremely nasty—to go on a difficult journey. It's a medieval concept derived from pilgrimages. Suffering is implied, for to travel in the year 1375 was to suffer indeed. But it was seen as a transformative suffering, an escape from the boredom of daily life. Later, the notion of travel as an improving exercise emerged in the Grand Tour of the eighteenth century, as enjoyed by young British gents. The Grand Tour was entertaining, but it was not supposed to be. Nor did it entail venturing into the unknown. It was a cultural pilgrimage to the known world.

But over the next two hundred years, a curiously wild and romantic conceit took hold of the Western itinerant. Once upon a time, there used to be two kinds of places: those you hadn't been to personally, and those that *nobody* had been to. Accordingly, there were places like Venice and Rome, which the Grand Tour had always taken in, and then there were primitive jungles, desert islands, remote peoples, and exotic cultures that remained mysterious and inaccessible. Tourism, as it became a multinational industry in the nineteenth century, began to trade in both these kinds of places simultaneously. It did so for obvious reasons. Tourism is always looking for new frontiers and novel experiences— which it then immediately liquidates. The colonial system of that century, made safe by British gunships, made the "primitive" enticingly available for the first time. It was only a matter of time before such primitives (inhabiting the most tourable Edens) were brought into the tourist fold.

In the twentieth century, the two kinds of places became deliberately confused. And it is this forced mixing up that has resulted in what I have called "whereverness." It is almost as if a plurality of different kinds of places—some known, some unknown, some civilized, some wild—have been flattened into a single kind of place that tries artificially to maintain all those qualities at the same time, while achieving none of them. The impoverishment is catastrophic, yet since tourism is consensual it is difficult simply to disdain it. All one can do is record its strange, unprecedented whereverness.

This is why I think it must now be said that travel itself is an outmoded conceit, that one no longer travels in the sense of voyaging into cultures that are unknown. Travel has been comprehensively replaced by tourism. But tourism itself is so improbable, so fantastical, that this process is almost impossible to grasp unless one takes a moment to look briefly at its history. For, as I have already suggested, the modern tourist is the descendant not only of the pilgrim but also of the Grand Tourist and the organized travelers of the imperial age. How, then, did this evolution occur?

The term "Grand Tour" was first used in Richard Lassels's *The Voyage of Italy* in 1670 and described an informal journey through the Continent for young British aristocrats, who were usually accompanied by a tutor called a bear leader as they made their way through a galaxy of cultural attractions in France, Switzerland, and Italy. The Tour, as it came to be known, arose because of the new wealth of the English, which made them Europe's most affluent tourists, but it also expressed an uneasy cultural inferiority complex, a need to

Europeanize the manners of their uncouth progeny—their "raw boys," as Tobias Smollett called them. The journey took months and was meant to inculcate taste, to improve "worldly manners." In 1749, the scholarly antiquarian Thomas Nugent wrote a popular guidebook called *The Grand Tour*, in which he laid forth the principles of the Tour as follows: "to enrich the mind with knowledge, to rectify the judgment, to remove the prejudices of education, to compose the outward manners, and in a word to form the complete gentleman." The aim was connoisseurship, an appreciation of beauty (the word "connoisseur" entered the language at about this time), but also worldliness, urbanity, what later came to be known as cosmopolitanism. For a nation that was emerging into imperial dominance, it also gave vent to a parallel superiority complex. The British were the ugly Americans of the early eighteenth century.

"The Tour," the British historian Ian Littlewood comments, "gives a pattern to what has remained the standard form of culturally approved tourism. Today's guidebook, with its lists of monuments and its advice on local purchases, is a direct descendent of Nugent's."

The destination of preference was Italy. Before Egypt was made available in the nineteenth century, Italy was to the British the epitome of civilization embodied mystically in a national landscape. But Italy was not a simple attraction. Venice and Naples were the Bangkok and Manila of the Age of Enlightenment. Venice was the prostitution capital of Europe, and the young gentlemen knew it: the absorption of Renaissance art went hand in hand with whoring. Daniel Defoe wrote in 1701: "Lust chose the Torrid Zone of Italy, / Where Blood ferments in Rapes and Sodomy."

Outside of the official literature, the Tour became synonymous with a breakdown of Britishness, a sexual disintegration. Long before Dr. Arnold instituted the praeposter system at Rugby, a supposed rise in homosexuality in England was imputed to travel in Italy, referred to in tracts as "the Mother and Nurse of Sodomy." James Boswell's intimate diaries during his travels in Italy in 1764 show how the Grand Tour actually looked on the ground—a cornucopia of hookers and horny countesses. "I'm determined," he writes, "to try all experiments with a soul and body." In Naples: "My passions were violent. I indulged them; my mind had almost nothing to do with it. I found some very pretty girls. I escaped all danger."

Italy was turned by this deluge of "raw boys" with cash into the world's first truly tourist nation and its great cities into the first subtropical tourist metropolises. (In the nineteenth century, tourists were known in Italian simply as *inglesi*.) This could never have happened without prostitution, or without the reputation for sexual ease that eventually lured English women as well. Connoisseurship, art, manners, education, and sex made the Grand Tour a fertile model. Its two most important contributions to the idea of tourism were the building of a continental travelers' infrastructure—hotels, restaurants, brothels, stage coach lines, theaters, etc.—and then the idea of a personal self-transformation through the simple act of moving through foreign climes. The tourist was seen as a malleable, impressionable subject upon whom all kinds of sublime improvements could be worked, usually with the aid of antiquities and sunshine. He was not a fixed human work but a piece of wet clay upon which sensations, learning, and ecstatic experiences could be impressed as easily as marking it with a scalpel.

Thus the tourist, the great-great-grandchild of the Grand Tourer, has never regarded himself as *complete*. He thinks of himself as unfinished, imperfect, in the process of rapidly changing as a foreign culture bombards him with stimuli. He is an unstable subject as well as an impressionable one.

Since the Grand Tour, travel itself has been seen as morally dynamic and transformational, not a dreary and static necessity imposed by diplomacy or trade. Consequently, the tourist cannot help but see himself as a pilgrim in search of revelations. And it was only a matter of time before this strange mentality was transferred onto the rest of the world. For as soon as the British had conquered most of it, they simply made the Grand Tour global.

The first place outside of Europe that they turned into a new Italy was Egypt. Egypt had long enjoyed cultural prestige, but it was far more inaccessible than Rome. Not only was it Muslim, but its levels of disease and insalubrity made it a logistically forbidding proposition. Imperial expansion solved this dilemma. With the Mediterranean now controlled by the Royal Navy and Ottoman hostilities subdued, the scene was set for touristic distractions of a highly organized and genteel nature. Above all, it was made safe for female travelers and children. The masculine pursuits of Flaubert and Maxime Du Camp in the 1850s, a wonderful mixture of onanism and amateur photography, were rendered moot by the arrival of boatloads of British families with nannies and servants in tow, expedited from London by the newly founded Thomas Cook and Son tour company and now lodged at a palatial hotel with hot and cold running water.

Thomas Cook, the founder of modern tourism, turned Egypt into a fashionable winter resort for the British middle class in the 1870s and 1880s. Thomas Cook himself (1808–92) had turned his family business into the world's greatest travel agency, and in 1870 the Ottoman viceroy in Egypt, Khedive Ismail, had made him the official agent for Nile traffic. But it was his son, John Mason Cook, who became manager of the London HQ in 1865, who set up offices throughout the Empire and in the United States, thus globalizing its operations, and who concentrated on Egypt as his premier destination.

The turning of Egypt into a British protectorate in 1882—the Veiled Protectorate, as it was known—opened up a tourist paradise for the Cooks. Almost immediately, they secured a monopoly of luxury Nile cruises, which they had invented, and the Nile quickly became known as "Cook's Canal." The company offered a set fare from London to the First Cataract of £119, all included. It was a whimsy of the rich, however; a British worker's annual wage in 1880 was about £60. For the upper middle class, it could be around £800. The trip took six days.

Cook's opened hotels in Aswan and Luxor, some of them medical to attract the therapeutic winter sunshine crowd. The monopoly was extraordinary; the army that sailed down the Nile to rescue General Gordon in 1884 went on Cook's steamers. Soon, the imperial authorities had granted Cook's mail and government travel monopolies as well—a perfect example of the symbiosis between empire and tourism. Aswan became the "Cannes of Egypt," yet another British social scene, and in 1891 John Cook estimated that tourists were spending £4 million a year in Egypt. Luxury hotels appeared everywhere—the Mena House near the Pyramids, the Khedival Club and Shepheard's in Cairo, the Turf Club, the Gezireh Palace—many of them still in operation. And Cook's capital rose to over £200,000, half of its profits coming from the Nile alone. By 1900 there was a vastly cheaper "popular Tour," with trains, hotels, and ships all included for about 40 guineas. (They had already invented the traveler's check in 1875.)

It was a remarkable cultural revolution. Apart from the thousands of Egyptians who learned English by working for Cook's, the European visitors were also shaken up into novel combinations. The English traveler and Egyptologist Amelia B. Edwards gives a typical description of the dubious tourist types crowding Shepheard's Hotel after she arrived there in November 1873, "literally, and most prosaically," as she puts it, "in search of fine weather":

> It is the traveller's lot to dine at many table-d'hôtes in the course of many wanderings; but it seldom befalls him to make one of a more miscellaneous gathering than that which overfills the great dining-room at Shepheard's Hotel in Cairo during the beginning and height of the regular Egyptian season. Here assemble daily some two to three hundred persons of all ranks, nationalities, and pursuits; half of whom are Anglo-Indians homeward or outward bound, European residents, or visitors established in Cairo for the winter. The other half, it may be taken for granted, are going up the Nile. So composite and incongruous is this body of Nile-goers, young and old, well-dressed and ill-dressed, learned and unlearned, that the new-

comer's first impulse is to inquire from what motives so many persons of dissimilar tastes and training can be led to embark upon an expedition which is, to say the least of it, very tedious, very costly, and of an altogether exceptional interest.

His curiosity, however, is soon gratified. Before two days are over, he knows everybody's name and everybody's business; distinguishes at first sight between a Cook's tourist and an independent traveller; and has discovered that nine-tenths of those whom he is likely to meet up the river are English or American. The rest will be mostly German, with a sprinkling of Belgian and French. So far en bloc; but the details are more heterogeneous still. Here are invalids in search of health; artists in search of subjects; sportsmen keen upon crocodiles; statesmen out for a holiday; special correspondents alert for gossip; collectors on the scent of papyri and mummies; men of science with only scientific ends in view; and the usual surplus of idlers who travel for the mere love of travel, or the satisfaction of a purposeless curiosity. (*A Thousand Miles Up the Nile*, 1877)

Edwards perfectly describes the aimlessness and airiness of the imperial tourist, for whom the world was not so much an oyster as a delightful wrong turning. "For in simple truth," she admits, "we had drifted hither by accident, with no excuse of health, or business, or any serious object whatever; and had just taken refuge in Egypt as one might turn aside into the Burlington Arcade or the Passage des Panoramas—to get out of the rain."

Edwards's book gives us Oriental scenes that are always "charming" and "picturesque." But it is also built around a series of archaeological encounters evoked in incredible detail. Many tourists shared her avid antiquarian interests, yet despite the Victorian seriousness with which they tracked down ancient steles, the pleasure of this kind of travel was also insular and social. The British liked to refind each other during set "seasons" on the Nile and in set hotels. The season in Cairo was from November to spring.

Tourism's motley crowd were the vanguard of an eventual colonial conquest, for in the case of that unhappy land it could be said that tourists occidentalized an Eastern country only a few years before the gunships moved in. It was for this reason that nationalist crowds burned down Shepheard's Hotel in 1952. They saw the connection clearly enough.

From the beginning, the same connection was at work with the 1869 Suez Canal, which was placed under British guardianship by the Convention of Constantinople in 1888. Egypt was never a formal colony and the canal was a "neutral zone," but even before the British had bought out the canal's Egyptian shares in 1875, it was critical for the opening up of India and Southeast Asia as tourist destinations. With a shipping lane now cutting quickly through to India, the Grand Tour could be extended considerably. The crowds on the Shepheard's Hotel verandah could now disperse economically across the rest of the Empire.

As the new tourist route flourished, the London-to-Sydney run (taking in places like Aden, Calcutta, Singapore,

Bangkok, and Bali) became fashionable. But, as Amelia Edwards shows, a "tourist" was not necessarily a single type. He or she could be a con man, a scholar, an amateur watercolorist, a criminal on the lam, a coxcomb, a minor poet, a honeymooner, or, more improbable, an anthropologist.

There is something about this route, which later became known as the Asian Highway to the hippies of the '60s, that is suggestive, attractive, even though today it is never pursued in a boat. If there is one travelers' axis that explains the whole evolution of modern tourism, it is this one. However, I didn't particularly want to write a social history of tour groups. The Asian Highway was desirable for the purposes of my escape because it had been followed by so many seeking the same thing—a route to some kind of "end of the world."

But this world's end was not Australia, which was after all Anglo-Saxon and familiar. It was first Bali and Indonesia and then, when those had worn thin a little, the huge island of Papua New Guinea. The journey had distinct phases. You set off from Southampton or New York; you passed through the familiar landscapes of the Grand Tour, namely the classical Mediterranean; then you arrived in Egypt. You passed through the Suez Canal to Aden, then—as if leaving classical civilization behind—you passed into "the East." First the Gulf, then the Indian Ocean. Many tours stopped in Bombay and Calcutta before reaching Penang in Malaysia and Bangkok. From there, the routes shot southward into yet more exotic spheres—the Dutch East Indies.

The Dutch Indies stretched from Jakarta to the western half of New Guinea, and in the beginning of the twentieth century as tourism was opening it up, a smattering of anthropologists traveled these same boats to arrive at places that were supposedly "unknown."

Before anthropology became a dry academic career zone, its pioneers were among the most serious and poetic of travelers. Margaret Mead's *Letters from the Field* and Claude Lévi-Strauss's *Tristes Tropiques* are classics of travel writing, even though Lévi-Strauss begins his book with the imperious declaration, "I hate traveling and explorers. Yet here I am proposing to tell the story of my expeditions." When I was traveling, so to speak, professionally, both Mead and Lévi-Strauss were constant companions in countless lonely hotel rooms. But they always gave me a bad conscience. So this was what real travel had been like in 1925, or 1935, or even in the 1940s. Both writers emanate a fierce sense of loneliness as they wander, and of adversity. They give the impression—which may be false—that they had reached the edge of the West's infrastructure and simply stepped outside it. They are winding narratives of personal discovery.

I identify easily with the twenty-four-year-old Margaret Mead setting off for Samoa in 1925 from Philadelphia, as related in the *Letters*:

I had the courage of almost complete ignorance. I had read everything that had been written about the Pacific Island peoples who had become known to the Western world through Captain Cook's voyages, and I was deeply interested in the processes of change. But I myself had never been abroad or on a ship, had never spoken a foreign language or stayed in a hotel by myself. In fact, I had never spent a day in my life alone.

"Whereas the tourist," Paul Bowles wrote, "generally hurries back home at the end of a few weeks or months, the traveler, belonging no more to one place than to the next, moves slowly, over periods of years, from one part of the earth to another." It's a great definition—but you could also say that it defines the difference between a tourist and an anthropologist. Thus, although I am not especially interested in anthropology, I began to find myself drawn to places that anthropology still held as in some way "outside."

In *Tristes Tropiques*, Lévi-Strauss describes his desire to find what he calls a "Lost World." Having completed some fieldwork among the Bororo people in Central Brazil, he begins to cast about for a more dangerous, radical journey and to find more uncontacted tribes. The anthropologist, indeed, must always be susceptible to this treacherous romance— that of a region, a people, lying beyond the so-called known world. In Brazil, Lévi-Strauss thought he might have found this magical promise in a remote region of the northwest plateau that had been incompletely explored by General Cândido Mariano da Silva Rondon in 1907. The report of the Rondon Commission, as it was called, was the only information available on this wild land stretching between Cuiabá and the Rio Madeira, though a quixotic telegraph line had been run through it in anticipation of its becoming Brazil's next El Dorado—for it was reputed to be rich in diamonds. The boom never happened. By the time Lévi-Strauss got there, it was an eerie, abandoned place marked only by the poles and a track next to them known as the Rondon Line. On either side lay mysterious forests where a people called the Nambikwara lived:

> Anyone living on the Rondon Line might well believe he was on the moon. Imagine an area as big as France, three quarters of it unexplored, frequented only by

small groups of native nomads who are among the most primitive to be found anywhere in the world, and traversed, from one end to the other, by a telegraph line.

What drew Lévi-Strauss to the Nambikwara, the heart of his book? Was it because before them "the observer is taken back to what he might easily, but wrongly, consider to be the infancy of the human species"? More likely, insofar as I can reconstruct it, it is a traveler's emotion, the craving for a mythic place beyond known time and history. The Rondon Line was straight out of a García Márquez novel, with its fantastical dialect composed of forty words fused from Portuguese and Nambikwara, its telegraph operators sometimes discovered buried waist-deep by the Nambikwara and riddled with arrows, their Morse keys placed on their heads. I have no idea what professional anthropologists think of Lévi-Strauss today or whether any of his work concerning the Rondon Line holds up after half a century. What interests me is the unconscious emotion that carried him there.

The history of anthropology suggested another place similar to the Rondon Line. In 1935, Margaret Mead set off from New York with her glamorous British husband, the scientist Gregory Bateson, on a tour of East Asia organized by the Dutch KPM shipping line. They had met on New Guinea while doing fieldwork and now were traveling on the glitzy KPM Dutch steamship line, which had pioneered organized tours into the Indies, especially Bali—it was KPM that commissioned the island's first tourist brochures.

In Bali, Mead found a Dutch colony with a Hindu caste system, a secretive culture unknown to the outside world that she could study as a pioneer. It was part of a swath of Asian Islands used as case histories in her work: Samoa in 1925, the Admiralty Islands in 1928, Papua New Guinea in 1931–32, Bali in 1936–38, and Papua New Guinea again in 1938.

Mead's work culminated in Papua New Guinea, where she found all the material she needed to overturn what she perceived as the patriarchy, racism, and puritanism of her native America. In 1932 she studied three peoples in northern New Guinea called the Arapesh, the Mundugumor, and the Tchambuli. It was her classic study of these three Papuan peoples in *Sex and Character* that laid the foundation of today's "gender studies" by seemingly proving that the roles of men and women could fluctuate wildly even within a relatively tiny geographic area. (Among the Arapesh, for example, women were aggressive and dominant while the men were passive.) But it also turned Papua New Guinea into the anthropological lab of the twentieth century.

Papua was the end point of the Asian Highway. Few actually went there, however. Unlike Bali, it didn't have intricate Hindu temples or comfortable gardens; it had no city comparable to Bangkok or Singapore. It was dangerous, difficult, but for Mead it incarnated a primitivity that was going to reveal everything about civilization. And meanwhile Papua had been discovered as a place unlike any other: a window into the human past, an island sealed off from the world, or even *out* of it.

It was Mead's chapters on Papua that charmed me most. She had stayed in a village on the Sepik River, where shamans conducted crocodile hunts and the children were painted with rose-tinted mud from head to foot. A picture of innocence seemingly out of time. One wonders what inner desire drew her there. It would not be far-fetched to say that it was the same desire that drives the manic traveler. The thirst for otherness, for evidence that we are not universal or even normal. *That* was precisely what Mead wanted to find.

For by a weird loop, the primitivity of Papua lyrically rendered by Margaret Mead—an immensely popular and influential figure in the United States—must surely have entered the subconscious of a baby boomer generation bent in the 1960s on swarming across the planet in buses, planes, and boats, seeking an antidote to the West. The spiritual East, the innocent savage: they are ancient conceits, as we shall see. But their current vogue has a great deal to do with both tourism and Margaret Mead.

Yet unlike all the other stops on that once fabled Asian Highway, Papua has stayed wild. Almost nobody experiences it. There are few "attractions"; the malaria is encephalitic. Civil war rages in the rain forests. Rumors of head-hunting and cannibalism can be more easily dismissed by the intellect than by the heart. And so, perhaps inevitably, I began to think of Papua.

New Guinea is the world's second largest island, about twice the size of California. With the innocent racism of the sixteenth century, the Portuguese named it *papua* to denote the "fuzzy hair" of its indigenous inhabitants, who likewise reminded later arriving Spaniards of the Africans of Guinea. It is artificially divided into two countries. The eastern portion is officially named Papua New Guinea, independent from Australian rule since 1975, while the western half—a Dutch colony after 1828—has been ruled by Indonesia with an iron hand since 1969 under the bogus name of Irian Jaya (it is actually an acronym), now amended to Papua, though West Papua is sometimes used for descriptive purposes.

The differences between the two Papuas are striking. PNG, as it's known, is anglophone, with a pidgin language called Tok Pisin (the pope, for example, is gaily translated as "Jesus Number One Man"). It's also considerably more developed, with a greater invasion of Ph.D.-chasing anthropologists drawn by fragile once-neolithic cultures. Isolated by a dragging war of independence against Indonesia, Bahasa-speaking West Papua is a very different matter. Police permits are needed for travel into the interior, where violence occasionally flares up and suspicion of foreign visitors is acute. Apart from the coastal capital of Jayapura and the world's largest gold mine near Freeport, there is little in the way of infrastructure.

The southern rain forests are among the wildest places on New Guinea, devoid of roads or towns, unvisited even by Indonesians, rife with rumors and legends. It was here that twenty-three-year-old Michael Rockefeller, scouring the coast for Asmat art in 1961, was reputedly killed and eaten by cannibals—a probably bogus tale that Conrad would have relished. The missionary Alfons van Nunen, who worked in Papua for fifty years, once wrote of cannibalism that "this practice has been extinct for years." But then, as Conrad also wrote, "people love the abomination."

New Guineans speak more than a thousand languages, a sixth of those spoken on earth. With a population of only two million, West Papuans speak 251 of them. Many are virtually unknown to ethnography. Papua's fauna is similarly profuse, perhaps the richest plant life on earth. More than 120 genera of its flowering plants are found nowhere else, and there are 2,770 species of orchid alone, but there are no monkeys and no large predators apart from the giant salt-water crocodile. There are bizarre tree-climbing kangaroos, the world's largest butterflies and pigeons, and 800 species of spider.

Before a civil war erupted in the 1990s, a few visitors made their way into the Central Highlands and especially the town of Wamena. But then tourists began to be kidnapped. From out of those same forests a shadowy "liberation army" emerged, headed by warriors with Shakespearean names like Titus and Goliath. The OPM (the Free Papua Movement) declared a desperate guerrilla war on the Islamic superstate that had appropriated them through a UN mandate to which Papuans themselves had never agreed. Its leader, Moses Werror, led them into jungle battles with mobile militia units of the Indonesian military called Brimobs—forgotten savagery far from the court of world opinion.

The Brimobs sometimes swept down from the skies in helicopters, torched a few tree houses, slaughtered everyone in sight, and left as suddenly as they had arrived. In the forests near the border with PNG there were known mass graves of people who had been killed simply for a thing called "flag raising"—that is, illegally raising the Papuan independence flag, the Morning Star. It was this undercurrent of secretive violence that had eventually destroyed Papua's tourist trade and emptied the two or three hotels in the tribal capital of Wamena.

———

And yet Papua has become the ultimate destination for a new breed of traveler, what could be called the "anthropological tourist." Small firms have popped up to cater to their very particular needs, with names like Hidden Cultures and Primitive Destinations International. The slogan aimed at wealthy Americans and Europeans is often "Back to the Stone Age!" (*Zurück in die Steinzeit!*) Anthropological tourists are a sophisticated variant of the ecotourist. They are not anthropologists by any means, but they share the anthropologist's ethos: subtle, invisible contact with fragile and remote peoples, extreme sensitivity, a light touch.

Primitive peoples can even be concocted by tourism ministers. In 1971, a Stone Age group called the Tasaday were supposedly discovered in the Philippines' South Cotabato province. Wearing only leaves, they appeared to be living in caves and using only stone tools—or so a Marcos minister named Manda Elizalde claimed. A hopeful American media descended at once. In 1972, *National Geographic*, in a classic noble savage story on the Tasaday, showed a naked boy climbing a vine with the Rousseauistic caption, "In naked innocence, a Tasaday boy toys with a bright bloom plucked from the wilds of a primeval Eden."

But anthropologists quickly claimed the story was a hoax. The Tasaday, they said, had simply been persuaded by Elizalde to go into the forest and put on a few leaves. The area was promptly cordoned off by the government, but in 1986 after Marcos's fall, the Tasaday were found wearing Levi's and living comfortably in houses. Had they ever been neolithic?

Papua is different, but only certain parts. Along the southern Asmat coast, deep inside the Yanimura and Sepik rivers, in the high inland valleys of Wamena, a Papua of flat-tened images ekes out a living as a spectacle. The Dani peo-ple of Wamena perform pig-killing ceremonies in their compounds, knowing that a rare visitor wants them to look wild: like the pulsating tusk-laden natives inhabiting the is-land of Bali Hai in that 1949 LSD-like piece of camp, *South Pacific*. With its psychedelic color moods and sex-war songs, Rodgers and Hammerstein's musical provides the closest thing to a mass-produced image of the Papuan male savage; although the film is supposedly set in Polynesia (and the ac-tresses look Balinese), the men seem to have been lifted by an art director from a *National Geographic* issue devoted to the Dani—and indeed the first *National Geographic* piece on Papua had appeared in 1941. With its hazes of rose and lime, its angelic singing, and its absurd mountain constantly changing color, Bali Hai was a no less strange glimpse into a musty compartment of the Western imagination.

Like Bali Hai, Papua itself has never seemed *in* the world. The first outsider to reach Wamena in 1938, the American aviator Richard Archbold, wrote in his notes that the ten-thousand-year-old Dani terraces "looked like the farming country of Central Europe"—but on the ground the people looked far more unreal to the incredulous visitors who be-gan to pour in. Naked except for their penis gourds, covered with pig fat, pig tusks, and cowrie shells on their bodies, their faces painted black. By 1938, Africa was colonized in its entirety and neat white farms dominated the landscapes of Kenya and Rhodesia; Polynesia was Europeanized; the Amazon spoke Portuguese and Spanish. Papua was, and is, the last Lost World. And there is nothing the West loves more than a Lost World, an image of Utopia.

Web sites devoted to Papua travel are numerous. It's an easy enough place to visit if you are content to join an Indonesian tour based in Bali and complete a swift circuit of five or six highlights in helicopters, speedboats, and minivans. Here, essentially, is the problem. From Bali you can fly easily into Jayapura and from there into Wamena. The national carriers Garuda and Trigana will take you there. To the Indonesian company promising "wonderland Stone Age sensations" and "primitives living happy in big garden" you will pay about $2,000 for a ten-day or two-week whirlwind tour, sleeping in "nice hotels" that will not be nice at all and busing into predetermined villages where predetermined ceremonies will be laid on for you. The Web sites show a kaleidoscope of images that subliminally portray Papua as a merry part of Indonesia, for the boar tusk fellows are elided with the little girls of Bali with gold turrets on their heads and the sunsets of Seminyak Beach. The subtext is not hard to grasp. Indonesians are terrified of Papua and of Papuans. The latter are black, they are not Muslims, they eat pork, they regard themselves as conquered, and they dislike Indonesians. No Indonesian company will take you past Wamena, into the dark hinterland beyond. I made a few e-mail inquiries about doing so.

"Not possible," the replies came. Their implication was that the forests were not fit for human enjoyments, but, more than that, that they did not represent a tourist objective that could be understood. It therefore falls to Americans and Germans to organize these penetrations of the farthest edge of the human world, which is also the farthest edge of the global touristic enterprise.

The sites of these companies are a very different matter. There are barely half a dozen of them. Many sport a heavily moralistic tone against tourism, the very thing in which they are engaged. The environment is defended, as are the "rights of native peoples," as if prospective clients might be hostile to either. The pictures are amateur digitals taken by the proprietors themselves: the faces of forest people, unexpressive and haggard, the psychotic blue heads of rare cassowary birds and tree houses sewn into a canopy two hundred feet high. There are a few pictures of men wearing penis gourds made of hornbill beaks.

The hard core of Papuan travel, the southern rain forests spread over a forbidding area east from the PNG border and south of the Central Highlands where Wamena sits encircled by glaciers. Wamena and the Dani are easy pickings; every travel writer worth his or her salt has been there. But the forests are another matter. When I called a few anthropologists to ask what region of the world remained off their map—understudied, little frequented—they mostly agreed that it must be the sago swamps and rain forests of southern Irian Jaya. For anthropologists, permits to work in this part of Papua are tricky to get. The Indonesians have finally caught on to the fact that American academics are always sympathetic to a liberation struggle and that in their writings they have nearly always cast the Jakarta government as the villains. And then there are the costs. Doing fieldwork for a year in the world's wildest forest is not cheap, and anthropologists are always underfunded. The military are unsympathetic to them, and many of the Dutch missionaries have abandoned the struggle to keep their landing strips open in the jungle: out there, the Christians have finally understood, you are on your own.

A German company promised a tour of the remote tree houses of the Korowai people near to the Yanimura River. A German tourist had died there the year before, so business was a little slow. But the river would not be as wild as the core forest, anyway. Because wherever there is a river there are boats—which means missionaries, traders, and tourists.

Internet gossip revealed that around Yanimura, tour operators sometimes asked the Korowai to change out of their T-shirts and shorts, put on hornbill penis gourds, and climb into the traditional tree houses in time for the *Zurück in die Steinzeit* tour from Stuttgart. According to anthropologists, the Yanimura was turning into a foul mini-Klondike as Chinese and Javan traders appeared looking for rare *gaharu* incense, tropical birds, and timber. There were whorehouses, ramshackle villages, tourist boats. It was being annexed to the great amorphous shit hole puzzlingly known (according to an obscure French economist) as the "Third World."

To get beyond the Yanimura, I had to find a guide, and there were only two or three in business. But, in the end, there was one who stood out. I had seen his name here and there, along with the sobriquet "the White Papuan." The White Papuan? He was named Kelly Woolford and he ran a one-man company called Papua Adventures. The White Papuan was a forty-year-old native of Missouri who lived in Ubud in Bali. From this "cultural capital" of Bali, Woolford set off on his manic trips into the heart of Papua. For Jayapura is only a four-hour flight from Bali and of course it is part of the same country. I began to correspond with Woolford. On his site there were more pictures: a group of Kombai of the Merauke forests gathered around a tall tree house with their bows, a wretched bivouac with three exhausted faces peering out. One of them belonged to Woolford, with a graying beard and a ponytail. This was one of the "tree house trips," and the men were eating around a small crude fire. "It's not an expedition for the fainthearted," he said in one missive. "You're going to the last wild place, the *edge*."

Who were the Kombai? I called Rupert Stasch at Reed College, the foremost expert on the neighboring Korowai people. I asked him about the Kombai, but he admitted that almost no fieldwork had been done on them. No monographs, no books, no full-length studies. There was a limited dictionary of their language—in Dutch. Since I do not read Dutch, I could not read anything about them or their culture. I could discover merely that there were two thousand of them, that theirs was one of the world's least spoken languages, and that they were obsessed with witchcraft. Were they like Lévi-Strauss's Nambikwara in some way?

For the November 2004 excursion, we would be based at first at the abandoned missionary station of Wanggemalo. Godforsaken is a much overused word, for does God really forsake actual places? But Wanggemalo was thus. The Dutch missionaries left in 1994; it was said they had made only one convert. I would be going with three European scientists. There was a *rassemblement* in Bali, so that we could fly out of Denpasar airport together. I had thus my end destination; all that was left to do was find some way of imitating that once ponderous Voyage into the East that would lead up to it—a simulation of the long, reflective sea journey that had taken generations of other white idlers to the Indies. For if you want to find out what kind of tourist you are—which is

to say what kind of traveler, what kind of *human being*—
you have to dawdle as much as you can.

Air travel has destroyed the rhythm of the long-distance
ship. The savoring of places that are hard to get to and that
are approached slowly—with a lot of vomiting on the way—
has vanished. The ship was like Mann's Magic Mountain, a
floating sanatorium where everyone knew everyone. But
now there is only the airport, which itself becomes more and
more hideous with every decade that passes. Even the airport elegance once incarnated by Eero Saarinen has disappeared, and so, one might add, has the leisure of the Grand
Tour, which usually took about ten months to complete. Instead, there is the frenzied crush, the anxiety of waiting
rooms, the lines at immigration, the boarding and disem-
barking at high speed. Consumer rummaging, electronic hysteria, the four-day minivacation, and the weekend package.
No one but the wretched travel writer has the time to take
off eight months.

But to delve into the tourist and his past, one has to do
just that. To reexplore the nature of a "journey," it is imperative to decompress the modern travel package. Airplanes
too can be used in an anachronistic way, so that the passen-
ger can tarry in place after place instead of rushing through
to a final destination. For even in the most absurdly acceler-
ated trip, the journey itself will count more than the destination: this is simply a psychological fact. That was the logic of
the Grand Tour, after all—that movement itself stirred and
awakened the soul.

Flying out of Dubai, I could proceed to Calcutta, then to

Bangkok and so on to Bali and Papua. In this way, I could pass through several phases of Easternness, all of them now touristified and packaged for visitors like myself, the harried escapists of a hemisphere so rich it no longer knows what to do with itself but *move*. It would be a panorama of modern tourism, a gaudy cross section of the charlatan global spectacle—and what portal into the upside-down world of tourism could be more gaudy, more symptomatic than Dubai?

INTO THE EAST

I flew into Dubai on a Tuesday night. It was starry over the Persian Gulf and inside Dubai International Airport there were two skies visible: one artificial and made of fairy lights, the other undeniably real and filled with what looked like supernovas. The airport is a model of modernity. Palm trees stand in geometric lines under a vaulted metal roof with huge porthole windows; this is sustained by metal columns ringed with "sprays" of gold lights and Arabian Nights arcades with night skies and sunsets peeping between lancets. The effect is of a giant Bedu tent equipped with escalators. The floors are palatially antiseptic. Emirates officials in white robes and headgear glide over them soundlessly, seeking out small children who are entitled to a kindly reprieve from the lines. Half the aliens in line were Chinese girls with imitation leather bags, already snapping open their cell phones and muttering in Cantonese. The mishmosh travelers usual to the Middle East were already abundant: Indian salesmen in bright checkerboard shirts of fantastical blues, Jordanians and Egyptians unshaved, masters of the histrionic sideways glance and saddled with bulging attaché cases, the British Family in Marks and Spencer shorts coming in for a week of beach and taxless shopping, Russian hookers in jumpsuits, the odd oil man standing out like a soldier at a disheveled tea party.

Dubai Airport, which was originally designed by the American firm of Page and Broughton, is a continually evolving piece of Orientalism honed to seduce seventeen million strangers who pass through a Gulf city-state of barely one million. Beyond immigration, a vast sala opens up, a consumer hive typical of those airports that have in recent years turned themselves into hubs. Hubs are more than airports. They are bazaars aimed at trapping what are called "transit consumers" with a cornucopia of retail outlets, restaurants, and wine bars. They are little cities unmoored from place and time, utopian wherevers that form the joints of an emerging tourist civilization. In Dubai, the facilities put any American hub to shame. Glass-roofed restaurants of terrifying grandeur calmly accommodate smoker and non-smoker alike. (It used to be called tolerance.) Caviar and smoked salmon are on the menus, expertly made espresso, reasonable champagne: all the things that the Wherever Hub Airport provides to its grateful children. You can get measured for a suit, buy a Maserati, eat soft-shell crabs, equip your pad with carpets, and do the laundry. Theoretically, you could do all this on your way from Paris to Bombay, in the space of two hours. It is the third biggest airport retail concession in the world and probably the most hedonistic. Before leaving, I slumped into a wine bar and drank three glasses of Mâcon-Villages with a Honduran cigar—it helps the jet-lagged wanderer sleep, because I had in fact reached my destination. Dubai is the fastest-growing tourist destination in the world, a portal of the New Middle East, and the white tourist has not been exotic for many years. People pass you by indifferently, glancing over quickly merely in order to check out the quality of your shoes.

The Dar Al Sondos hotel is run by the Le Meridien chain on Rolla Street in the neighborhood known as Bur. It was relatively spartan: Russian tour groups stayed there alongside Indian sales reps and a few tourists from Turkey. Around the hotel stood patches of desert covered with green tufts of drinn, Saharan grass, and walls defining empty development lots. Sand blew everywhere. Rolla is an Iranian immigrant street and that is what its restaurants are. In their windows sit the sad pale men in exile from across the straits with bundles of mint on their plates, staring out into a relentlessly commercial middle distance. There is always a subtle rage about Iranians. Chinese hookers go past with the usual gaiety of Chinese hookers, swinging garish "designer" bags and offering to their clients names like Min Min and Lucky Ann.

I couldn't have explained why a mood of low-key paranoia gripped me as soon as I arrived at the Dar Al Sondos Apartments. Perhaps it was the sudden appearance of traveler's solitude in a place where no provision is made for it. From my little cement balcony I could investigate dozens of apartment windows on the opposite side of the street inside which black-robed women leaned over rice cookers and bowls of laundry.

Unable to sleep, I went to one of the Iranian cafés. Soon, I was one of the pale men in the window with a bundle of mint being waved to by the Chinese hookers. I began to feel liberated. After months of claustrophobic confinement in New York, a moralistic and corporate city, this single street

in the East, Rolla, seemed airy, relaxed, with a whiff of the
Mad Hatter of course, but that is a whiff I can accept. I
waved back. Boatlike white Mercedeses coasted past, their
number plates adorned with a small image of the Burj Al
Arab hotel and their windows tinted. A few doors down
stood the Imperial Suites hotel and nightclub, where wealthy
Arabs went to find Uzbeki models. On the sidewalks, the
male faces were mostly Tamils, their hands whitened from
construction cement—Dubai is only twenty percent Arab,
and most of its inhabitants are from India, an army of imported hoplites who build the marinas, the hotels, the banks,
and the theme parks. They walk around in gangs, staring
into the white glare of the camera shops.

At the end of Rolla lay a much larger avenue lined with
multistory electronics malls and parking lots filled with pros-
titutes. Turning left, I wandered into the junction of
Sakhoun and Marsheer, which is filled with global brand
billboards and "gentlemen's hotels." On the far side stood
a glass-fronted establishment called the York Hotel with a
steep flight of steps. Chinese women in tight satin dresses
tottered down it. Crowds of Indian men stared longingly at
them. I barged into the bar and ordered a Black Russian,
hoping to insult someone.

Dubai nights are interminable, with no beginning or end;
the whole place has been invented as a feudal enclave to
make aliens happy. The bar was filled with Russian girls. A
Russian air crew sat at the bar on sticky stools, smoking tin
hookahs. A surreal sunken lobby could have belonged to the
Berlin of the '30s. Whores asleep in armchairs, men from
Turkey and Lebanon dozing with their rings and cigarette
holders. A nightclub upstairs. If you ask for a room at the

hotel, as I lost no time in doing, they smile, look away, and say it has been booked six months in advance.

On toward the Creek, the turbulent river that splits Dubai city in two. The streets like a giant canteen lit up, crowded with minimarkets, curry cafés with outside tables where Tamils smoke away over their dals. Tailor shops with Sikhs ribboned with measuring tapes, dusty apartment blocks with cracked letters. It was surprising that a vital seediness had been left intact inside so swanky a city, like the seediness that exerted its "deep appeal" over Graham Greene when he strolled through 1930s London:

> . . . the seediness of civilization, of the sky-signs in Leicester Square, the tarts in Bond Street, the smell of cooking greens off Tottenham Court Road, the motor salesmen in Great Portland Street. It seems to satisfy, temporarily, the sense of nostalgia for something lost; it seems to represent a stage further back.

Greene is right, seediness is a taste of the past, nostalgia for something lost. There is nothing more exasperating than reading in contemporary guidebooks disparagements of places that are deemed to be "seedy." Do the writers not notice that such places are invariably crowded with people? When a neighborhood is described as "seedy" by some *Lonely Planet* prude, I immediately head there.

The Creek is a wonderful river. I am sure it too used to be seedy, but at least it has kept its mercantile swish and hustle. The old souks, the walls of the fort and mosque still bear down on the wharves, which are cleansed and lightly airbrushed now. The river curves sharply. You could be in

Shanghai or Suez. Banks and minarets rise from the far side, which is called Deira, shadowing motorized dhows and water taxis covered with yellow bulbs. At the north end of the Creek, I passed a mock Bedu village. A few scraps of sand and an old man blowing onto a fire. Tourists stood around, solemnly taking his picture. At the other end of the river esplanade, the old Persian quarter, the Bastakia, is now remodeled to resemble a theme park, its narrow alleys lit with soft orange lamps too tastefully embedded into the flagstones. The wind towers look half ruined, but they have been contrived to look that way. By nine in the evening, the place is like an abandoned film set. Thus, the city's historical quarter looks more modern, more mall-like than the malls that are themed to look like historical sets. One cannot tell the Madinat Mall and the Bastakia apart. Everything has been telescoped into the eternal present, which is after all the preferred dimension of the tourist.

It is often said, not only by the chamber of commerce, that Dubai is the ultimate "tourist city." Since I had a few days to kill here before flying out to Calcutta, I wondered how best to use the time. I could go to the elite restaurants, the beaches of Jumeirah, the splendid themed malls like the Wafi and the Renaissance, the famous girlie nightclubs like Cyclone mentioned in every Bachelor's Guide to World Travel. But did Dubai have an essence that could be discovered in only a few days? The city-state is surely a social laboratory in which a new model of resort living is being tried out. And it is true that Dubai's ruler, His Highness Sheik Mohammed bin Rashid Al Maktoum, is masterminding an extraordinary gamble: that he can turn the 2.4 million tourists who visit Dubai every year into 15 million by 2012.

To do this, he is using two construction companies that he largely owns, Nakheel and Emaar, to reconstruct the city-state from the bottom up. The new city will have the world's tallest tower, the Burj; the world's largest shopping mall, the Emirates Mall; and the world's largest theme park, Dubai-land, intended to be larger than the surface area of the actual city. Yet more incredible, however, is Nakheel's plan to build three gigantic artificial palm-shaped peninsulas sustaining a galaxy of hotels, resorts, gated villa communities, and enter-tainment districts. The Palms will jut out miles into the Per-sian Gulf and will be visible from outer space. It is very important for Maktoum, apparently, that his pet construc-tion projects be visible from outer space.

Next to these Palms, moreover, they are building an en-semble of 250 to 300 man-made islands that together form a vast map of the world—for each island will be shaped like a country. The islands will be sold to developers who will then, it is hoped, build something unique on each island ap-propriate to the island's "nationality." A mini-Mecca hotel on Saudi Arabia; an Eiffel Tower cinema on France. The project is called the World.

Images of these tourist fantasies are everywhere in Dubai. They have become part of the city's future subconscious. It would be interesting to know what Margaret Mead would have thought of them, or if they could be subjected to an an-thropology of any kind. Do they express kinship structures or a cosmology? An idea of power or pleasure? By the road one sees gigantic images of Sheikh Maktoum, the Builder, the modern Nebuchadnezzar of the Gulf. The sheikh's eyes follow you everywhere and they are not merry. It seems obvious, then, that the Palms and the World are expressions of power. And these are just part of the story. All along the coast road, self-contained "cities" are springing up, a Media City, a Knowledge City, a Science City. As if each function of the state could be given a separate neighborhood with a wall around it. In any case, I thought I might as well try to visit the World and the Palms. I had an acquaintance in Nakheel's PR firm, a local company called Orient Planet. He is a young Lebanese exile called Khudr Hammoud, who likes to call the Palms the "most significant" project in the entire Middle East, if not the entire planet. Evidence of the Arab nation being reborn, though as yet there isn't much to see. The Palms and the World are still construction sites.

"I still want to see them," I insisted.

"As you like. Afterwards, you can go have some fun. I have the phone number of an excellent Chinese girl. I recommend that you bring her flowers. Chocolates are at your discretion."

Producing the publicity for Nakheel is a daunting operation, for it amounts to selling Dubai's image to the rest of the world as a hyperglobalist metropolis that is both fantastical and real: a city-resort with a working mercantile infrastructure. For Khudr turned up a little disheveled, as if he had been at an all-night party, and ten minutes later we were speeding in a company car toward the Palm Jumeirah. On the way, we passed the whole length of Sheikh Zayed Road. Its parade of avant-garde skyscrapers decorated with heads of the sheikh struck me as Mad Hatter enough, but Khudr seemed intensely proud of it. Progress, brutality, power. What did I think?

"Amazing," I said. "Very modern."

Ah, we are not as backward as you thought, eh? the eyes said.

But I was not thinking any such thing. I was wondering where Maktoum had gotten the idea to create such monumental avenues lined on both sides by such massive side-by-side towers. The diaries of Mussolini? A trip to Miami? It was an Easterner's touristic idea of the West.

It is one of the great themes for a writer: what one culture wants from another. Predictably enough, we were soon talking about the Iraq war, and Khudr was giving me the standard resentnik line, uttered however with great feeling and bitterness. His argument could be summed up as, "We don't want your so-called values, we want *this*, the gleaming skyscrapers and the babes that go with them." He used phrases like "the poor Arabs." Shafted by the West, driven from their lands by unreasonable Zionists. But at the same time Dubai was "the future of the Arabs," because it was not inferior to the West in the quality of its interstate highways and malls. Americans were rather disgusting and oafish, a terrible lack of culture, basically, but he'd rather like to spend some time in New York seeing if he could hustle up some business education.

"New York must look something like this, no?"

But over there, he insisted, the Jews controlled everything.

"I suppose they must censor everything you write. That's the way it is. Here we say what we want."

We arrived at the Palm. It was little more than a giant's causeway of leveled sand and dirt projecting into the sea under a mass of cranes and arc lamps. Thousands of workers in yellow hats swarmed around what would soon be a freeway coursing down the middle of the "bole" of the seven-mile-long Palm. And for a moment I did think of what New York must have been like in 1930, a place in a blind frenzy of self-making.

We drove around for half an hour trying to find the Nakheel motor launch that would take us out to the World. Khudr and the driver argued in Arabic as we passed blocks of unfinished villas. Finally we stopped at a jetty surrounded by water clotted with yellow foam. At its end lay a spotless white launch, splendid with navy cushions and tumblers of chilled scotch. The personnel saluted as we stepped aboard. Khudr playfully tapped my arm. That's the life, eh?

The Palm is difficult to describe, unless you happen to be sitting above it in a hot-air balloon. From sea level, it looks like a network of desert islands, mounds of white sand, sitting on a topaz sea. Twelve thousand real palms will shade its streets. These will be grown in a special nursery in mainland Jumeirah. There will be underwater marine parks, Hyatts and Hiltons, and, probably, Jean-Georges and Nobu outlets—the whole machinery of tourist splendor. And just behind the Palm sits the Burj Al Arab, the world's most expensive hotel, shaped like a dhow sail on the Jumeirah waterfront. The three Palms together will increase Dubai's beachfront by some seventy-five miles, three immense "dreamlands" given over to the logic of twenty-first-century leisure. Naturally, Nakheel calls the Palms "the Eighth Wonder of the World." One could call them a scene of wonder. We drank our scotch numbly. Why does the world have only *eight* wonders?

Khudr had the boat swing close to the Palm's shore. A

jungle of scaffolds and cranes shimmered just above the waterline. The first villas were being built. I was beginning to wonder why millionaires would choose to live on a giant artificial palm tree in the middle of the sea. Khudr pointed over to the Madinat Mall, on the Jumeirah shore, built to imitate an ancient Gulf city, complete with faux mud towers bristling with wood poles and crenellated walls. Its ominous silhouette sat just above the water: a mall looking like a restored ruin, or vice versa. A canal flowed through it, a canal with boats and promenades. Very jolly. A bit like the mad village in the British TV show *The Prisoner*.

"Fantastic," Khudr said. The other men nodded gravely.

So this was the new East. Just like the West, it was now imitating itself.

It seemed a long time since the first Western tourists arrived in "the Orient" looking for picturesque poverty and ruins, courtly scenes with water pipes and harems of tattooed slave women. Now they came to buy second homes with Oriental themes that only lightly alluded to the former image repertoire. Accordingly, the Palms will soon offer a selection of grandly themed residences, Garden Home units in a Sante Fe style, as well as Arabic, Greek, and Mediterranean. Interiors will be lavish, a riot of marble, columns, and stupendous chandeliers. Canals, docks, and beaches will permeate every neighborhood. The floating city will soon look as utopian as resort living can, an Ideal City worthy of Plato. But who will live there? No one seemed to know. Khudr looked at his notes and brochures. No, there was nothing about buyers yet. "Europeans, Saudis," was all he said, but what he really wanted to imply was the global middle class, for there will soon be one and it will be five hundred million strong.

The World lies two and a half miles out to sea, the sandy isles shaped like various countries in sizes ranging from 250,000 to 490,000 square feet and priced from about $11 million to $36 million. There's a France, a United States, an Italy, an Egypt, and so on. A hundred of them have already been sold. With rehearsed drama, Khudr let on that Rod Stewart had bought England for a tidy sum. He had beaten David Beckham to it, no doubt.

We steered a course between a group of these islands, passing so close to them that we could have jumped out and swum to shore in seconds. From close to, it was impossible to judge which part of the World we were navigating through. "I think," Khudr ventured, "it's Africa. I think this island over here is Saudi Arabia. Yes, it's Saudi. There's Oman."

We slowed the launch to look at Oman. It did not look at all like that opulent and mysterious land. There was a fire hydrant standing in the middle of it. Farther on, we passed India and then swung toward Australia. Once, it took weeks to sail to Australia, and who would want to? But here you could sail there in five minutes. True, there might be an obnoxious Lebanese millionaire living there who might tell you to get off his property, but the notion of sailing was still pleasurably exotic. And in fact we were now sailing along the Asian Highway itself, the Margaret Mead route as I now call it. Just north of Australia I asked Khudr if he could show me where Papua New Guinea was. The word, however, meant nothing to him.

"Papua?" the staff wondered.

"It's the world's second largest island," I said.

Khudr: "Never heard of it. I'm sure we don't have it."

"It's an important country not to have."

I then told him that I myself was heading to Papua. This necessitated some explaining: what Papua was, how big it was, what kind of people lived there, and, lastly, why I was going there.

"Sounds like a fucking awful place." He smiled. "If we had a Papua New Guinea, how would we market it? Who would want to buy the Papua New Guinea island and live on it? That's why they didn't build one, I suppose."

The logic was faultless. I couldn't quite imagine Rod Stewart making a bid for Papua New Guinea. Would one have to build tree houses on it?

We skirted Japan and made our way back to the Middle East, where Egypt beckoned—a prize island over which many a sheikh would doubtless be haggling. I then asked an incredibly naïve question: "Where's Israel?" For, like Papua New Guinea, it appeared not to exist.

"You mean Palestine?"

It had been left out for reasons of "tact." We sailed through the gap where that triangular little island would have stood, and there was a moment's unspoken heaviness. So the World was not quite the world.

"If we *had* an Israel," Khudr finally opined, "who would buy it? It would be an Al Qaeda magnet. No thanks."

A little farther on, we came to a sprawling white villa being built for the United Arab Emirates' defense minister. The house already had its sunproof blue windows and steel balcony rails, as well as a grove of young palms with tightly bunched fronds. A Caterpillar tractor sat nearby with a group of Indian workers. A house rising from the sea, then, surrounded by ocean on all sides—the ultimate in planned seclusion. I looked around at the desertlike hillocks of bare sand and tried to imagine what it would look like in ten years' time, forested with hotels and villas and swimming pools. Then Khudr informed me that, if I wanted, I could visit the Nakheel HQ and see all the master plan maquettes for the developments. They were expecting me after lunch, in fact. He talked into his cell phone for a few minutes as we voyaged back to the jetty, and our second view of the Jumeirah skyline gave me a more oppressing feeling—I could not help being reminded of the skyline of Coney Island at the turn of the century, all pagodas, towers, and spires, a mock-up of the eventual skyline of Manhattan. Why do people build such things? Parody has a more powerful hold on the imagination than reality. Which is tantamount to admitting that tourism is more powerful than reality.

As if chiming in with my mood, Khudr suggested I go to lunch inside the Madinat Mall before heading on to the nearby Nakheel HQ. It was the best mall in Dubai, some thought, though there were so many themed malls these days that it was hard to say. The Madinat had restaurants, in any case, that were popular with Dubai's movers and shakers. I could also buy a carpet and an Armani suit if I wanted.

Khudr adjusted his tie and looked furtively at his watch. Did he have an amorous rendezvous somewhere?

"Hamza Mustafa of Nakheel will be waiting for you at HQ. Don't be late!"

The car left me at what looked like the gates of a walled city. The mall is entered through a monumental gate, its towers bristling with traditional wooden poles. It could easily be a restored archaeological site, or an "old town" surviving intact for centuries. For a moment I wasn't sure that this was *not* the case, and it took a few minutes to verify the absolute modernity of the construction. For inside, the streets are covered like an ancient souk and vaulted in traditional woods. The sunlight enters in broken bars and spangles, iron lanterns hang from the beams, and the storefronts are framed by massive carved wood doors with Hand of Fatima knockers. Many a Sinbad Antiques sits in picturesque shadow. It is a perfect piece of Orientalism, but this time it has been made by the East itself.

The Madinat contains a hotel, villas, and a canal bordered with restaurants. After passing through the Souk I came into the open "city center," with its square Gulf-style towers, piazzas, and palm groves. From this core, a labyrinth of gates, courtyards, and covered shopping arcades, only the mall's own skyline can be seen; the wharves are shaded by café parasols and palms, the water's reflections dominated by the pale pink of simulated dried mud— the traditional building material of the Gulf. As I walked around this mise-en-scène I couldn't help thinking of an operatic set, and of course more than any other opera this set would resemble that of Verdi's Egyptian-themed *Aida*.

In *Culture and Imperialism*, Edward Said takes a scathing look at the "falsity" of *Aida*, which as a theatrical spectacle, he says, confirms "the Orient as an essentially exotic, distant, and antique place in which Europeans can mount certain shows of force." Verdi's opera pretended to look like a genuine Egypt, but of course it was nothing of the sort. It was rather like a model village at a colonial Universal Exhibition: a spectacle of "subaltern cultures . . . ex-hibited before Westerners as microcosms of the larger impe-rial domain. Little, if any, allowance was made for the non-European except within this framework."

But what about the mall I was now standing in? It seemed to bear the same relation to archaeology that *Aida* did. Unlike the sets of *Aida*, moreover, this is a vital part of an Arab city in which an Arab middle class goes about its daily business. Its spectators are indigenous.

Said appears to think that every Westerner is condemned to have a colonial psyche. But what he seems not to have considered is that a people can Orientalize itself, or that in fact it *principally* Orientalizes itself. The pisé towers around me were the Arabs romanticizing themselves. The two hours went quickly as I became more and more disarmed and alarmed. Little canal boats with awnings went by, the Mid-dle Eastern families looking at the towers with binoculars. A helicopter landed on the distant Burj Al Arab helipad, where Andre Agassi had just played an exhibition game that morn-ing as part of the Dubai Open. I thought to myself: Yes, I have a colonial psyche, but who does not?

Hamza Mustafa is the head of Nakheel's sales division. In traditional robes and headdress, he sweeps with royal au-thority through scale models of the Palms and the World fol-lowed by a minion bearing a silver coffeepot. The coffee is strongly scented with cardamom, and Hamza's English is scented with British intonations picked up during a school career in the Somerset countryside. He is the sophisticated face of the new Dubai: smoothly debonair, armed with statistics, and equally at home in two world languages. We walked slowly around the fantastical models of the Palms showing how they would look when completed. The Palm Jebel Ali boasted a ring of boathouses inside its crescent, which formed—when seen from outer space, of course—a gigantic Arabic poem.

"Written by our great sheikh. Isn't it nice?"

It was about horses, he said. And he translated.

Dubai now allows foreigners to buy freeholds, and it's the resulting property boom that is fueling Dubai's growth. But the forces of global tourism are, in any case, favoring Al Maktoum's wildly grandiose visions. As Hamza is all too aware.

I got an expert peroration about tourism. "Today's tourism is driven by climate. Sun and sand weighed against the miserable winters in Europe. We realized that Dubai simply didn't have enough beach—a measly forty miles. The palm tree structure enables us to construct thousands of villas all with beach access. And to double our beach area with one stroke. Do you see? It's really quite ingenious. The palm is the perfect *commercial* as well as aesthetic structure." He said this as if these two things had never before coincided.

Around us, other metal palms soared up to a tentlike roof. Receptionists in black robes and headscarves floated through a maze of glass sales offices from which a group of property developers from a company called Zenith exited murmuring in several languages simultaneously. They made straight for the Palm Deira model, taking digital snapshots as they went. Hamza broke off for a few minutes to give them an authoritative spiel, which amounted to saying, "This, ladies and gentlemen, will transform world tourism!"

Then he took me to the World. In the model, the islands were covered with bizarre structures, fantasy hotels and Miami-style villas. Hundreds of tiny white yachts lay moored by miniature jetties. I thought to myself how deliciously nightmarish it would be if the whole thing suddenly came to life.

"We also realized," he continued, "that since oil was only six percent of our revenues and falling, we had to diversify. Tourism is the world's biggest industry. And tourism itself is changing. A lot of our clients from places like Britain want to live here part of the year. Forgive me, but your climate—" He opened his hands wide, as if to suggest that Allah had not favored my race in that department.

But where were the clients coming from?

"From all over. The U.K. mostly. Then Hong Kong, India, Germany. Some from the U.S., but on the whole we find that Americans are terrified of the Middle East. It's possible that Atlantis might change that."

Atlantis? Hamza's eye turned black mischief. The ruthless South African entrepreneur Sol Kerzner was building a version of his Atlantis theme hotel and casino on one of the Palms. I said I had been to the one in the Bahamas—a megaresort devoted to the legends of the Lost City, complete with an invented hieroglyphic script and underwater restaurants.

"Very magnificent, is it not? Atlantis will make people think of the Bahamas. And we are certainly going to overtake the Bahamas."

I looked around the opulent glass-and-steel "tent" and picked up a dozen languages in bits and pieces. The multilingual murmur rose and fell, a background noise sounding like an ur-language from the distant past. The word "multicultural" is on everyone's lips in Dubai. Another project of Nakheel's is International City, a complete miniature city rising in the Al Warsan district with whole districts themed by region and dominated by a thing called the Forbidden City—a 240,000-square-foot replica of the Beijing original.

Hamza sat me down and had coffee poured into a cup so tiny I had to hold it with three fingers. He asked me how long I was going to be in Dubai.

"And after?" he asked, with genuine curiosity.

"East. India, then eventually Papua New Guinea."

The urbane smile was a little chilling. "So you are quite the adventurer, are you not? I cannot think of any reason for going to Papua New Guinea, I must say. Did you know they are building an Islamic University in Papua? I have heard—perhaps I am mistaken—that the Saudis might be involved in financing it. In Wamena, I believe."

"It is amazing how *large* Islam is, isn't it?"

He looked over the models, where the Europeans were stroking their chins and thinking about their checkbooks.

"Your trip is taking you from one end of Islam to the other," he said. "But then I go shopping in London on the weekends. We have all the stores here, but I prefer to go to Savile Row myself."

I drank some of the burning coffee. Across the polished marble floors, incredibly beautiful women floated on stiletto heels, their heads garbed in black. Hamza pointed at the model of the World, and a forced sincerity entered his eye.

"Our great sheikh has it all planned. The world will soon be traveling all the time, round the clock. And Dubai will be the center of it all. To go to Asia, Europeans will come here first. Like you did. And like you, they will stay a few days.

Since you are here for a few days, I advise you to go to the Wafi Mall. It is sublime. Excellent wristwatches, too. And of course you should not miss the Burj Al Arab."

Returning down Sheikh Zayed Road, I had to admire the giant images of the sheikh's face looming under spotlights, undulating on flags and pennants and billboards. The logos of his construction companies, Emaar and Nakheel, were posted like the propaganda banners of two rival political parties. The glass towers were straight out of Alphaville, evidence of a benevolent dictatorship whose aegis permits a planned multiplication of pleasures. For we have forgotten how far dictatorship and pleasure can go hand in hand—how often, in fact, they depend on each other. If a dictatorship could provide hedonistic outlets, while refraining from using electroshock therapy on its journalists, it would have a high chance of enjoying the gratitude, admiration, and perhaps even envy of most of the world, not to mention its own citizens. It is a recipe that has made Dubai and Singapore rich.

Like a British lordling on the Grand Tour two hundred years ago, I went the following night to see the Venetian-themed Mercator Mall, which looks like a Renaissance train station filled with sheikhs carrying shopping bags. There are *gallerie*, arcaded streets with names like Via del Lago, squares with orange trees and frescoes of Venice in a style of imitation Canaletto. Then, instead of Cairo and the wonders of Giza, there is the Wafi Mall, with pharaonic statues guarding its gates and a pyramid of colored glass whose friezes are derived from the walls of Egyptian tombs. The following day I would be flying to Calcutta, the largest city ever built by Europeans in the tropics, and I wondered what version of "the East" it would offer in contrast to the one proffered here. For you could not find two cities more diametrically opposed within the tourist system than Dubai and Calcutta. The former was clean, much visited and admired, while the latter was seen as decrepit and shambolic, and was consequently hardly visited at all. How ironic it was that the British families whose ancestors built Calcutta never go there now, as if to underline the fact that the East is something one can take or leave. When it gets too chaotic, too *Eastern*, it is dropped from the tourist almanac altogether.

Accordingly, only loners and Japanese businessmen go to Calcutta now. And yet what city resonates more deeply in the colonial psyche? What city is more out of our world and yet in it?

SAD TROPICS

A little potbellied man with a straying left eye, like a character out of *The Pickwick Papers*, showed up for breakfast at the Calcutta Oberoi Grand, the vastest and grandest of the city's Raj-style hotel palaces. Manish Chakraborti squinted with his loopy eye, laughed as if with asthma, and plopped himself down into a paisley armchair. "I'm dying for a cigarette," he gasped, "and I suppose we can *not* bloody smoke?" Manish is the city's most impassioned architectural historian and the man most responsible for turning many of its listed buildings into UNESCO sites. As a sideline, he gives tours for the curious and the bored, the footloose and the indigently curious. For today's Grand Tourists, in other words, who want to see Calcutta's half-forgotten, half-ruined cultural sites. Manish himself is the perfect man for so quixotic and outmoded a form of tourism. Perfect English, vast erudition, a dim sadness behind the drifting eye: he dreams of resurrecting the decayed British city into a tourist mecca. It will probably never happen, but while it doesn't happen Manish will show the city to the kind of traveler who responds to lifelong love. He will show it stone by stone.

Calcutta's decay enraged Manish precisely because it was

so purposeful. Calcutta, and Bengal itself, have long been Communist principalities. Calcutta's walls are the only ones I have seen outside of Italy that are relentlessly plastered with hammers and sickles, not to mention exhortations to the proletariat. In the taxi coming from the airport, I had passed statues of Marx and Engels on the Maidan, the sweeping central park laid out by the British. The Communists were the problem, according to Manish, as they were everywhere else. It was they who had let the city slide into phantasmagoric ruin. A city whose texture reminds you of the decalcomaniac surfaces of Max Ernst's wartime paintings.

"Shall we have breakfast?" I said.

You can still see the Indian aristocracy's love of hand-blown Belgian chandeliers in the Oberoi lobby, for there they are, stalactitic masses of tubular antique glass with fifty flames gathered at the end of what look like pendant palm trunks. The hotel is set back from the manic colonial boulevard known as Chowringhee, now a squatter camp–cum–street market, and its serene courtyard is protected by squads of guards in glistening white uniforms and peaked caps. I was curious about the Oberoi itself, and not surprisingly Manish had its history at his fingertips. It had been the private neoclassical mansion of a wealthy Anglo-Indian family of the 1840s. A strange period, he said. The British had founded Calcutta in the 1690s, but the Raj had not been the continent's dominant power for very long when the two sides of Calcutta—British and Indian—began to merge at the higher echelons.

The British were riddled with racial paranoias, as we all know, but they made a hierarchical distinction between the "high" cultures of the Middle East and Asia and, say, the unredeemed primitivity of Africa or the South Seas. Contempt for the Indians they actually dealt with coexisted with respect for the cultural India of the past. For that matter, the British had brought the same psychosis into their Italian tours. They often loathed the Italians of the eighteenth century—whom they saw as degenerate—while in virtually the same breath they lavished praise on this *other* Italy of Hadrian and Michelangelo. In India, the same drama played itself out.

But with time, as in Italy, the cultural respect began to open other doors. In the 1770s, Governor-General Warren Hastings based in Calcutta had launched a campaign to revive Hindu learning (Calcutta had already produced the first English translation of the *Bhagavad-Gita*, by Charles Wilkins); a few decades later, rich Indians began building amazing palaces in the reigning European styles, filled with statues of Napoleon and Meissen candlesticks. Cross-fertilization began to flower.

It was this cross-fertilization that fascinated Manish. The mid-nineteenth century coincided with Calcutta's heyday, when it was the biggest and richest city in Asia. Comparisons with the present were bound to induce nostalgia, and wasn't nostalgia Calcutta's preeminent mood, the mood of her own artists and poets?

I looked through layers of glass doors and windows to the Oberoi pool, alive with hummingbirds in the early morning. Two blond girls swam lengths; they were members of a Thai Airways flight to Frankfurt that had been diverted to Calcutta because of a cracked windscreen. They looked extremely confused by their surroundings, as if Calcutta was only a swarm of little ideas: Mother Teresa, City of Joy,

Patrick Swayze. And then rickshaws, leprosy, child prostitution, beggars. Hadn't Woody Allen once declared that the city had a "hundred unlisted diseases"?

"You see," Manish said, "they are not here because they want to be."

The Calcutta of palaces was not for them. Like many middle-class Calcuttans, Manish hated the image the city has had fabricated around it, the Mother Teresa slum shtick. But had the vaunted Indian economic boom really reached Calcutta?

"The number of street beggars is about half what it was," he protested. Though he had to admit that the famous trickle down of wealth had not trickled down very much.

"The owners of the historical palaces are all broke. Everyone is broke. Including me, I am broke."

Manish gave his tours for 350 rupees a head, about $9, but it was of course a loving participation for him—opening his city to others. It is an ideal form of tourism, a personal gift from one person to another. Perhaps you can find it only in a failed city. For what would Calcutta look like if it had succeeded? Most of the old buildings would have already been torn down and replaced with Hard Rock Cafés. The sadness of Calcutta was of something beautiful protected by failure.

We went outside into the dawn. Manish got his cigarette and we climbed into a Hindustan Motors Ambassador with almost no brakes.

Early in the morning, the city looks like an equatorial Saint Louis of the last century. At its heart, like the temple of a departed deity, the white palace of Viceroy Curzon, modeled on his English country estate Kedleston Hall, stands amid lavish gardens, too big for its present function as the seat of the governor of Bengal. A hundred years ago, Manish said, it was almost matched by the Great Eastern Hotel on Sutter Street, the "Jewel of the Orient." We stopped there for a second. The Great Eastern was Calcutta's equivalent of Shepheard's, and it still takes up almost a whole block of Sutter. But the Great Eastern has been government run since 1975, and as every tourist knows, the terms "government" and "hotel" in India mix like oil and water. The lobby was dusty and decrepit; the once-elegant arcade was covered with billboards for sewing machines and ice-cream makers. Manish made a face.

"Scandalous!"

Like charioteers in *Ben-Hur*, we tore around the Maidan, where a dozen cricket games had started up as the mists cleared. We passed Engels and Marx again, and there was even a Ho Chi Minh Street. Was this compensation for colonial humiliation?

"It's stupidity." Manish snorted. "Like changing the name of the city to Kolkata. Or is it Kalikata now? You might as well advertise straight out that you have an inferiority complex."

There is no city as confusing as Kalikata. The British layout has been overwhelmed, though in photographs a hundred years back it looks utopian enough. There are no traffic lights; drivers use both sides of the roads simultaneously. The air chokes with fumes and there are times when nothing moves except the bicycles. I remembered Louis Malle's 1969 film about Calcutta, and what I recalled were Malle's collages of misery, which he seemed to have inherited from the aforementioned writers. If there was no misery there would be nothing to describe, to shoot. Calcutta is misery—we're all agreed on that. What does the tourist see, then?

The streets, no longer so wretched perhaps, the Rajastani mansions along a long street on the way to North Calcutta with their beautiful carved terraces and shutters of sooted wood; if you are with Manish you feel the palimpsestic density, like parcels that have been wrapped with sheets of paper from a hundred different novels of different epochs. I noticed most of all the faces packed into the Ambassador taxis as we stopped at intersections. The men leaning out a bit and asking where I was from. "George Bush, crazy man!" Thumbs up, gold teeth, a whiff of garlic. The girls looking like boxes of candies sitting in the backseats with fake gold fans and delicately sweated foreheads. The men being shaved under baobab trees; the feeling of a million desultory clerks asleep behind mountains of paper or sleepwalking from office to canteen and back to their pointless offices, where they chased flies with quills. Bureaucracy, bookishness, and aristocracy—for Calcutta is the supreme city of all three in decay.

The Manish Tour wends its way through the imperial heart of the city, taking in the British Gothica of Dalhousie Square and the Writers' Building, and then heads north for the decaying and preposterous palaces of the babu. The babu were Calcutta's original aristocratic families, few in number but adorned with gorgeous names. The Duttas of Hatkhola, the Tagores of Jorasanko, and the Debs of Sovabazar. They built their palaces under the British in the late eighteenth century, and thereafter they declined generation by generation, usually making a humble living as government clerks on their way down. They were, and are, remarkably bookish. Even during the Raj, however, "babu" was often a term of affectionate contempt, suggesting an Indian aping European fashions and manners, or else a poseur, a dandy . . . an intellectual. Manish opined that the Marxist government still wouldn't fund the restoration of babu palaces for political reasons. And so they slide into ruin, though Calcuttan palaces make for ruins unique in the world, the spectral twilight zone caught so gently in Satyajit Ray's *The Music Room*.

At the end of the day we visited the dying palaces in the northern part of the city, especially the famous Marble Palace, built by the babu eccentric Rajendra Mullick, who died in 1887 but who began the building when he was only sixteen, in 1835. We drove up to a gray Palladian pile next to which stood a dozy fish pool lorded over by a pelican. Next door, a rowdy mosque blared away as if to spite the minor babus who still own the palace. Some of these were asleep on the steps next to their discarded sandals. In the heat of the afternoon, we wandered around this shadowed semiruin in bare feet, padding over undulating marble floors where it was rumored an infant boy had been buried for good luck.

One wonders how these two cultures fantasized about each other in a mutual tourism of the mind. For the British, the fantasies of India were obvious and well known. But what of the other side? Indian fantasies of Europe are rarely glimpsed. The rooms of Mullick's palace are crowded with the same florid chandeliers sported in the Oberoi. Shrouded pool tables stand in one room; in another, a towering rosewood statue of Queen Victoria presides, regarded with awe by the old men following us around. It must have been fifteen feet high. In suffocating galleries, a Hercules crushing snakes by Reynolds and a scene of lusty Amazons by Rubens hung quietly degrading in the tropics. Around them swirled an orgy of Apollos, Neptunes, and scant-clad Venuses. One series of marble busts showed a young woman in progressive stages of marital fecundation: blushing virginity, prenuptial flirtation, wedding day, matronly maternity. The fierce sentiments of 1840. I pored over a statue of Napoleon and some blazingly tacky Meissen ceramics.

Clearly, the wannabe babus had latched onto something interesting in the Western psyche, and most of all the British psyche on tour. You could call it the life-as-a-museum conceit. It is the idea that a culture is a static storehouse of delightful curios, a maze of galleries filled with artifacts and rituals. The museum is therefore felt to be a microcosm of a real place—which, of course, it is not. Yet this is the operating conceit of the tourist. The Marble Palace is an instinctive Indian response to the antiquity-chasing British traveler like Amelia Edwards. It's almost as if they were saying, "You too can be hoarded, collected, touristified!"

It was dusk when I got back to Chowringhee. The boulevard was swallowed up with hordes: cinema crowds, market touts, arcade stalls laid on plastic sheets selling hand-cut seals, scuba flippers, coffeemakers, Nehru suits. A bluish haze rose from the park, where the cricket games continued under arc lamps; around the Peerless Inn next door, a male host milled in six directions simultaneously, carrying rickshaws and bicycles with it, the faces sweating in the fiery orange light of the road.

I went up to my room and my four-poster bed, exactly like a prince of the Grand Tour. The Raj antiques and prints

in the room, the wainscoted bathrooms, are corporate re-
constructions of a British officer's milieu, but they provided
a Western insulation against the frenzy of the street. In the
heart of a great hotel there is utter silence, an unreality that
stills the most frayed nerves. The sweat gradually dries on
your skin and your isolation returns. The hushed boys
padding along the carpeted corridors with their prints of
Old Calcutta, the swish of laundered saris and the polite talk
around the pool, where the gin and tonics are served to a
sound of parrots.

Tristes Tropiques is a loose collection of travels ranging
from the West Indies to the Amazon to Asia, between which
the restless Frenchman zigzags erratically by means of what
he calls "a mental tracking shot." He jumps from Brazil to
India and back because he feels like it. He is given to a certain oratory ("Alas, poor Orient!"). Otherwise, *Tropiques* is
written in a tone of detached indignation, of scrupulous ob-
jectivity and calm skepticism—which, in the end, are merely
the qualities of the pitiless eye and a roving ear. Mercifully, it
defies the humdrum demand of contemporary American edi-
tors to have a "coherent thesis," whatever that is. The
world, Lévi-Strauss seems to recognize, is not itself a coherent thesis, so why should it be interpreted through one?

But in the middle of this majestic work there erupts an
unhinged and delirious chapter on Calcutta under the title of
"Crowds." In it, we see the rage, disgust, and hysteria to
which even the anthropologist is prone, albeit displayed with
a rare candor. But perhaps that "even" is a little naïve. No
man is a mechanical camera.

What we are ashamed of as if it were a disgrace, and regard as a kind of leprosy, is, in India, the urban phenomenon, reduced to its ultimate expression: the herding together of individuals whose only reason for living is to herd together in millions, whatever the conditions of life may be. Filth, chaos, promiscuity, congestion; ruins, huts, mud, dirt; dung, urine, pus, humours, secretions and running sores: all the things against which we expect urban life to give us organized protection, all the things we hate and guard against at so much cost . . .

The key word here is "humours," as if Calcutta is medieval even in the medical sense. Lévi-Strauss then compares the human multitudes of India with the comparable emptiness of the Brazilian jungle. In the Americas, he says, one feels landscape acutely because people are small within it; in India, however, it is the reverse. The human crowds and a long history have obliterated nature, turning everything into human waste and exhaustion. The Indian city and the remote jungle are the two extremes of human experience that give the anthropologist his moral bearings. It's clear he prefers the jungle. Would I?

I do not, for the most part, agree with him about Calcutta. Lévi-Strauss spends an inordinate amount of time dwelling on Calcuttan hustlers, as if they were unlike anything he had ever experienced before. They seem to have gotten to him in an acute sort of way.

Every time I emerged from my hotel in Calcutta, which was besieged by cows and vultures perched on

its windowsills, I became the central figure in a ballet
which would have seemed funny to me, had it not
been so pathetic. The various accomplished perform-
ers made their entries in turn: a shoeblack flung himself at my feet; a small boy rushed up to me, whining
"One anna, papa, one anna!" A cripple displayed his
stumps, having bared himself to give a better view . . .
a New Market porter begged me to buy everything . . .
He listed the items covetously, as if all the goods were
presents intended for himself. "Suitcases? Shirts?
Hose?"

After reading this diatribe in my four-poster bed, I was
curious to know which hotel Lévi-Strauss had stayed in. He
mentions that it was a luxury establishment and that it was
around the corner from the venerable New Market, for that
was where he had suffered his ordeals. But the Oberoi
Grand was around the corner from the New Market and it
was, as far as I knew, the only old luxury hotel that was.
Had Lévi-Strauss stayed here?

Throwing down the book, I got dressed and went back
down to Chowringhee. The New Market lay on the block
behind the hotel, reached by a street of chemists and cloth
stores. It was thick with human bodies, and I had to swim
through them. The Market is also a British monument, but
soukified inside, so that as I wandered up the steps into the
first segment of the labyrinth I was lost at once and the "ballet" of which Lévi-Strauss had so bitterly complained began.
A hustler latched onto me, with a whole procession of facial
expressions that seemed to have been borrowed from a Peter
Brooks performance of the *Bhagavad-Gita*: woe, dismay,

surprise, anxiety, injured pride, incredulity, aggression, concern for his parents, concern for my parents, concern for my
children, concern for his children, etc. Street theater of the
purest kind, and of the kind that had driven the fastidious
European anthropologist insane. But it is after all only the
ballet of the tourist and his Other. A ritual that cannot be
avoided. My guide did what is customary in the New Market and bought us two beers while we sat at a gold mer-
chant's from whom he obviously got a commission. But
thereafter things got decidedly strange. Did I want to buy
gold? A firm no had him shaking his head, tutting with the
owner, a few swigs of beer, and then an offer to get us two
tickets from his cousin for the Elephant Festival at which, I
could rest assured, the Indians went mad and made for a lot
of good photographs. "Not wanting to go?" For I was shaking my head and laughing. It was Lévi-Strauss all over again.

But he suddenly got up and disappeared—to get the tickets for the Elephant Festival.

He came back twenty minutes later, cursing and shaking
his head. Couldn't find his cousin, couldn't get tickets.
Would I like some "girlfriend panty hose" instead? Under-
pants? Tablecloth? Our bottles clacked and I refused. We
started to chat about our respective lives, and he was keenly
curious. What kind of house did I live in, two floors or one?
Wife and kids? Why not? I learned a fair amount about him,
depressing as it was—he was a university student in "mechanical engineering"—and in return I described the insides
of the Oberoi Grand hotel. It occurred to me then that, apart
from desperately wanting to sell me things, he simply
wanted to have a banter over a beer with a foreigner.

By now I wanted to leave but could not figure out where

the exit to this incredible maze lay. He looked me over slyly. Then he said he could get me some Ayurvedic medicine. I didn't want any. "No, no, you will needing it!" His cousin had some freshly made powders. As I finished my beer, he disappeared again, this time for ten minutes, and I was already on my way out when he caught up with me, holding two dingy paper bags of yellow powder. "Sir, sir," he cried, almost kneeling, "take it, take the Ayurvedic medicine!" I had to repeat that I had no intention whatsoever of accepting his dismal powders.

"I understand!" he cried now. "You can pay me tomorrow. Or the day after tomorrow if you like! Here—"

And he thrust the paper bags into my hands. Now I was stuck with them and a look of complete, almost savage triumph came over his face.

"All right," I said wearily, "I'll pay you tomorrow."

"Yes, pay tomorrow, tomorrow!"

He bowed, I bowed, we began to move in opposite directions, and other hustlers closed in on me as I darted back into the dark arcades on Chowringhee. I was sweating violently, drenched from head to foot. The boys saw some look of weakness in me that had something to do with the two paper bags dangling from my fingers, with the traces of yellow powder that had begun to leak from them. Aha, they were thinking, so here is a jackass sahib who has had some Ayurvedic crap fobbed off on him. Very interesting! I wandered back into the Oberoi, quite confused as to what had just transpired. In the lobby, the bellboys stared at the packages as if they were miniature bombs, knowing of course exactly what they were, and I finally had to ask one to relieve me of them. They had a good laugh among themselves.

"Certainly, sir!" The condescension was so slight that it passed under my nose and evaporated. The packets were gingerly carried to a wastebasket and dropped into it with a smart brush of the hands. I was trembling, for some reason. As an Englishman I always feel that something is expected of me—but what? A show of rectitude, of stoic command? Or something out of *Trainspotting*?

What had happened in Calcutta was that the Englishness inside me had been evoked in a way it never had before. It is occasionally evoked in New York, but not as viscerally as in India. You are asked to play a part, a part that is fixed in the racial memory of others. For the tourist, it begins to get complicated. Which part of you is real and which is the part? In your own culture, you never think about it, but as a traveler you are forced to think about it all the time. Because in reality no one is ever taken purely as an individual—look at the way Western anthropologists look at Indians or, more extremely, Papuans. We are individuals, and *they* are "a culture." In the same way, for Indians I am an "Englishman," just as an American staying at the Oberoi Grand is always an "American." Push him a little and he will play the part, as will I. I just had.

For the next few days I wandered around Calcutta without Lévi-Strauss's disgust. Fewer cows than expected, no vultures, no pus. But the longer I stayed, the more it felt like a composite city assembled inside a single feverish brain, one of those fantastical Londonesque utopian scenes dreamed up by the Victorian painter John Martin. The Botanic Gardens with the "world's largest baobab tree," the ghats with their

Armenian baths, the strange industrial riverscapes of the Ganges with its chocolate-colored waters and hazy chimneys. I walked down Chowringhee and Park every night, shopping in bargain pharmacies, eating at Grain of Salt and Shish with the infotech hipsters, and dipping into the new American-style malls but never knowing where I was going or even where I was. For at least the author of *Tristes Tropiques* was right about the oppressive confusion of crowds. "Daily life appears to be a repudiation of the concept of human relations." But was he also right about the primitive forest being an antidote to the hideous "amoebic" cities of the modern world? Life is inherently easier and more dignified, he says, in places where people began to pillage only four hundred years ago, instead of four thousand.

I love cities. Or rather, I am inclined to be an urban tourist. When I walked across the Maidan in the morning to watch the cricketers set up their wickets, I felt that I was inside a nightmare to which I had taken a liking. No relatives, no friends, no phones ringing, no connection to anything: just the city teeming with birds and goats, with millions of strangers sleeping outdoors. At home and estranged in equal measure, the traveler picks his way through garbage and rubble to find a little peace, stopping to drink a milky chai at the street corners where the mango trees grow with mad abandon, their leaves shooting up among sooty architraves and rotted pilasters. But he is never really happy, for he is always thinking of his next move: like a billiard ball, he is motionless only temporarily. Always alone, it is his only comforting thought: "Tomorrow, I'll be somewhere else!"

DESERT ISLANDS

At Dum Dum airport, a small and mangy crowd had assembled for the two-hour flight to Port Blair. An hour before dawn, it was postponed and I went to look at the rain that was rolling in, for Calcutta is surrounded by estuaries, swamps, and lagoons, and its rain seems to draw energy from so much nearby water. There was now plenty of time for relaxed Indian conversations, for there seemed to be an unspoken complicity among all the people herded together for so obscure a destination. Almost no foreigners ever fly to Port Blair, the capital of the Andaman Islands, and a white fellow in a summer suit with a bit of jungle equipment rolled in ugly bags is bound to attract those grandfatherly queries from old men that cannot be turned away.

Five or six times I had to explain that I was on my way to a place called Papua New Guinea—no, it was not in India— and that I was flying to Bangkok first. Then, I explained, I had found out that halfway between Calcutta and Bangkok there lay these Andaman Islands and that I could stop off there on my way to Thailand. They nodded and their eyes shone. Did I know their history? How the British had built a terrible penal colony there? But, sir, all is peace and tranquility now. Except, of course, for the niggers. My chai nearly fell out of my hand. The what? Oh, yes, sir, the niggers. The Andamans are full of niggers. It was an old gent with a kind of origami piece on his head made out of a Bengali newspaper: rain gear.

"You will probably see them," he added darkly, "begging by the roads."

I was being disingenuous. It was precisely because of these remote tribal peoples that I was going to the Andamans. I had seen them first in an Indian newspaper article a few weeks before, where it was reported that in the wake of the 2004 tsunamis, the secretive hunter-gatherer tribes of the Andaman and Nicobar islands off the coast of Burma had fired arrows at relief workers in helicopters.

The Andamans are a long archipelago of some 572 islands that are mostly invisible on a map. They stretch north-south at about the latitude of Sri Lanka, lying closer to Burma than India. They were administered once from Calcutta before being turned into a separate Indian department and had belonged to the Indian Navy for decades. Only recently opened for tourism, they were devastated by the tsunami; their native peoples were Negritos, black Africans who had migrated across Asia seventy thousand years ago, and thus were related to Papuans, who were also Negritos. So, I had thought at once—astonished—it would be a taste of Papua before getting to Papua! They bore mysterious names, Jarawa, Onge, Sentinalese. Violently hostile to outsiders, they killed intruders into their forests. The British had built a penal colony there in 1858 because it was so easy to control the convicts: the Jarawa obviated any need for walls. Today, there were 238 Jarawa left amid 300,000 Indian settlers.

On the Air India plane, I was tense. There are times when the world seems nastily small; on other occasions it appears vast, cold, and very blue. I met the same old man at the back of the plane outside the toilets and, out of nowhere, he informed me that the famous "dumdum" bullet had been invented in 1889 in a small British munitions factory that had stood next to Dum Dum airport.

"You are, sir, a quite amazing people!"

There was no irony behind the spectacles, however—I wondered whether dumdum bullets had ever been used on the Andaman niggers. Two hours' flying time south from Calcutta, the islands suddenly appear out of a dark sea, sleeping like large beasts under mist and rain.

Descending into Port Blair, you could be flying into any logging town in the Amazon or, for that matter, Papua New Guinea. At least Papua as I imagined it to be, which was to say as I had seen it represented in the pages of the odious *National Geographic*. Sprawling hillsides of shacks and piled logs, networks of mud paths, corrugated tin roofs: an air of failure, of nowhereness, which is not the same as whereverness. It is a real place, you think, but a failed one, a half-place asleep in its tremendous obscurity and remoteness. Its charm has gone. It reminds you not only of Papua but also of Haiti's Port-au-Prince. Beaten-down trees, blue walls, the sea at the end of every alley. A skeleton of municipal respectability remains, a few lawns here and there, a ceremonial cannon peeping out to sea. But the living heart of it seems unsure in some way.

The airport was a bare warehouse. A deserted tourist booth offered a single leaflet listing three hotels, all in the capital. I took a leaflet to the exit and got a cab into town. It was raining with indescribable intensity. "Fortune Resort," I told the driver, and pointed to the little picture. We spun up hills at angles of sixty degrees, then rolled down them again—a fairground ride. At a roundabout I saw a black man wrapped in a blanket, his head covered with threads of red wool. The driver smirked.

The Fortune Resort Bay Island was designed by famed Indian "ecological architect" Charles Correa. It is in so-called Native Style, which is to say it offers airy pavilions with palm thatch roofs open to the sea, which bear no resemblance whatsoever to any Jarawa structures you will ever see. It is the top hotel in the Andaman Islands, which is to say that it is not owned by the government. The lobby is filled with Jarawa kitsch, paintings of happy black matrons and dancing children in red flower garlands, and on the verandah open to the sea stands a statue of a Jarawa warrior spearing his prey—a pig, or a passing tourist? The walls are covered with ecological propaganda, like a high school's: most noticeably, a picture of the "pollution system" of a Typical American City. Brahms's Third boomed on the sound system. I collapsed into a cane chair, and after about an hour a waiter appeared with a gloomy grin. He had a white napkin draped over his arm as if he had seen this in a training video. I ordered a gin and tonic.

"I am sorry, sir, bar is closed."

"Well, what time does it open?"

He looked at his watch. "In five minutes, sir."

He stood there smiling. I ordered the drink and said I would come back in five minutes. Then, neither of us left. He continued smiling. There was not a single guest in the hotel except me and another Britisher, who was sitting in the restaurant below, talking secretively into a cell phone. After five minutes, the waiter went off to get the gin and tonic.

I felt like the hero of *Dark Passage*, a man who has perhaps faked his own death. I peered over the railing to look at the man babbling into his phone downstairs. He wore a cheap "businessman" jacket and the voice was unpleasant. "We could go up to seventy-five," he was whispering urgently, hunched over a beer, "but I told him seventy-three, okay?" A jasmine-scented heat steamed the flesh, and lonely fishing boats crossed the darkening bay without lights. The end of the world, with Brahms.

The next morning, during another storm, I sent a message by hand to the governor of the Andaman Islands, Dr. Ramchandra Apse, couched in formal terms and asking if he could grant me a personal interview. I said I was a "researcher" and that I would like to explore the islands a bit. I knew that police permits were required to go "up island," which meant northward along the Andaman Trunk Road. The ATR, as it is called, cuts through four different islands, which are connected either by ferries or bridges. In some places it also cuts through the Jarawa tribal reserves, which was where the legal problems arose. For the Jarawa were strictly out-of-bounds to foreigners, and mostly to Indians as well. The government had long ago decided that in the interest of preserving their fragile culture they should be isolated from the outside world as far as was possible. They could not be met or even photographed, not even from a moving car.

It rained all day and I went for a wretched walk around the Aberdeen Bazaar, buying things like toilet paper, bottled water, and oranges. I had found a tour company that could hire me a driver, and he appeared at the hotel toward the end of the afternoon, a dashing youth called Vinod armed with a cell phone that took pictures. There was also a return note waiting for me from the governor's office. The great man, no doubt intrigued by my insolence, would see me that night. Would I come round for an interview—and tea?

Dr. Ramchandra Apse lived in a large white compound on the crest of a hill. It was obviously the former residence of the top British official, and slothful soldiers with ancient-looking Enfields loafed about at the entrance, which was guarded by two gold toy cannons. A secretary appeared and asked me to wait for a while.

Upstairs, on the first floor, a plump little satrap was waiting on a long navy sofa surrounded by ornamental elephants, fish tanks, and some portraits of Nehru and Gandhi hung high on the walls. Dr. Apse, professor of economics, former member of Parliament for Mumbai, was wearing a pale blue pajama suit and was talking with subdued ardor into a cell phone. It was hot and he looked a little sleepy. Suddenly he laughed and looked up: a pair of cunning, merry eyes shaded by owlish glasses. "I'll call you right back." He did not stand; his flip-flops remained as they were, but a woman in a pink sari, hovering indecisively behind a screen, gestured at a uniformed servant who suddenly sprang into motion. The phone rang again as I sat. "Hello?" the governor rasped, shaking the phone as if it was full of water. "Hello?" He looked at me: "See how it is in this place?" his eyes said.

The room was filled with model ships in glass cases. Moreover, there was an old British telescope, a giant conch shell, and a large picture of a tiger. The governor shook my hand and asked me, with charming care, whether I had enjoyed the flight from Calcutta.

"We are surprised to see you. After the tsunami, the tourists have dried up. May I ask which university you went to?"

The reply was apparently satisfactory, for he hunched his shoulders for a second and snorted. The governor dipped a biscuit in his tea, in the British way. He then dryly observed that at least the giant wave had put them on the map. The outside world had finally heard of the Andaman Islands by now. Or had they?

"I read the newspapers," I said.

"You read about the Jarawa. Everyone is writing about the Jarawa. It is the *Hindu Times*, sir. The *Hindu Times* is having a go at us. It is not the whole picture."

The *Hindu Times*?

"How we are having a problem with the Jarawa!"

Whereas, he continued, the Four Seasons chain had just bought an island here for themselves near Port Blair, and it was possible—likely, even—that the Andamans would be the next Maldives, the next Seychelles. "The Four Seasons," he suddenly cried, holding up his wet biscuit. "It is going to save the people!"

From what?

"From being poor. From having fishing for a living. Have you seen the fishing boats?" He got quite excited. "The Four Seasons is going to save them. And we *will* be the next Seychelles."

Who would want to be the next Seychelles? I thought dismally.

"Before being made governor," Dr. Apse went on, rather like a steamroller, "I came here as a tourist. I saw the potential at once. The beautiful sea, for example"—he searched for words, snapping his fingers as if the secretary might help him find them—"the different colors. Yes, the different colors. Many colors we are having in the sea. Very pretty."

The servants advanced again with their plates of fairy cake and tea glasses. The governor was now in an excellent mood. Perhaps it was the cake and biscuits.

Poverty. The pretty colors. They were grand themes, but what about the tribal peoples?

The governor let out an equally grand sigh. "Well, we cannot let tourists near them. Do not misunderstand me. We are all friends now. There have been difficulties in the past. But"—he shook his head, as if with superficial regret—"the Jarawa and tourism, they cannot mix."

But then I thought back to the Jarawa kitsch in the hotel. It was surely the other way round: the tourism industry was flogging the natives for all they were worth. The mood was now rather jolly, however. The fans cranked at full speed, the jokes flew thick and fast. He explained that in the Jarawa areas vehicles must travel in a scheduled convoy with armed guards. It was, I had been told, for one's own safety. The Jarawa were not especially friendly.

What he didn't explain was that poachers sometimes crossed over from Burma on contraband speedboats, seeking wild pigs, honey, and timber in the Jarawa's opulent forests. Their bodies were occasionally found in the jungle, nonchalantly slaughtered, though just as often the poachers simply disappeared and were never seen again. They meted out much the same treatment to Indian loggers intruding into their woods. In 1996, a party of armed loggers were ambushed by a large Jarawa war party—guns versus arrows. Two loggers were killed and three forest wardens were captured. The Jarawa later released them after cutting off their hands with an ax. In the last fifteen years there have been almost two hundred attacks on forestry and police personnel. In 1998, five Bengali settlers poaching in Jarawa forests were murdered. The Jarawa word for outsider, *eenen*, is often amended to *eenen piti piti*: "bad people."

The governor warmed to this chilling theme. "On no account can you stop and greet them. And on no account can you take a photograph of them. That, I am telling you, will land you in jail—"

Lightning suddenly flashed through the windows.

"Is it true," I asked, "that they cut off your hands if they find you in their forest?"

"Ah, many things have happened. You would be better off not stopping. I will tell your driver myself."

A slight irritability warned me that the subject should soon be changed. The Indians are very sensitive to accusations that they are bulldozing the natives into oblivion, as a colonial power would have done.

He changed the subject by asking what *I* was doing there.

"Researching," I said vaguely. "For a travel book."

"I am not sure what a travel book is. Surely you are not interested in the Jarawa? It would be better to write about the Fortune Resort."

The governor made a gesture of amused disdain. For how pointless it was to charge around the planet taking notes and putting oneself into all kinds of uncomfortable situations.

And where was I going afterward?

"Bangkok? A most fun city." Many colleagues went there for the fine Sikh tailoring and the most accommodating ladies. And then?

"Never heard of it," he murmured when I said Papua New Guinea. At least, not very concretely. Who were the Papuans?

"They are a little like the Jarawa," I had to say.

Dr. Apse's face tensed a little. "Then why are you going there?" He laughed.

"They have the last wild forests in the world. I want to see them before they vanish forever."

"We also have the last wild forests in the world. *And* desert islands."

There was a subtle colonial whiff to our interaction that I couldn't put my finger on. A jostling of some kind, a mutual taunting. It was obvious he considered my rationalizations for traveling little more than an idle Westerner's pretext for loafing about in balmy climes. And he was not, in fact, entirely wrong.

"But first," he said at last, "you simply must see our ruins in Ross Island. As a Britisher, you will appreciate them. Ross Island was the Britisher headquarters in the colonial time."

For a moment the governor looked like an old Polynesian king welcoming a seedy English captain to his shores. But there was a steel glitter in at least one of the eyes. Perhaps he was more like a British colonel, after all—a colonial bureaucrat serving out his time in some far-flung, godforsaken posting.

Downstairs, the guards snapped to attention and I was told that the brooding silhouette on the horizon was Ross, long abandoned and uninhabited, except of course by ghosts. Indians take their ghosts very seriously. It was better, they said, to go in the morning.

The morning boat to Ross takes a half hour. A mere two miles long and barely a mile wide, Ross is one of those many places once known as the "Paris of the East." Photographs from the 1880s, though, show not so much a miniature Paris as a bizarre re-creation of English suburban life at the heart of the penal colony—a kind of transplanted Tunbridge Wells with ficus trees.

From the jetty, you walk up through a palm grove toward a printing press standing like the ruins of a medieval monastery by the sea. Wild chital suddenly stop to watch you pass by. The ficus trees have multiple boles like massive barrel organs and inside the press their roots have exploded into a lattice that strangles the walls. Next to the press stands the Mineral Water Plant, its oxidized tanks filled with spiders, like futuristic cannons that have been mislaid. A path rises up the island's single hill toward a Jane Eyre church, tropical Gothic again.

It struck me that Ross is exactly what the ruins of our own megaresorts will look like in a hundred years' time. Ross had been a fantasy island, just as a Four Seasons island would be—the same exclusivity, the same illusion of tropical splendor carefully manicured and arranged. And, like a twentieth-century tourist resort, it had been utopian, a wild place rebuilt as a mini-England. There had been a barracks modeled on Windsor Castle, tennis courts next to which native bands played on Sunday mornings, a Christian cemetery, a grandiose bakery, officers' messes, ballrooms, and promenades.

But there is more to it than that. The British had built their empire around a string of naval bases, many of them islands. Is it any accident, then, that the British invented the romance of the "desert island"? Islands, that is, that are usually covered with dense greenery and bear no resemblance to deserts whatsoever. Islands "desert" in the old, appealing sense that they were largely uninhabited. They could easily be reworked into miniature paradises in the British image. Inadvertently, the British Empire had invented an extraordinary tourist concept: the self-contained tropical Western home-from-home, an island paradise sealed off from obstreperous natives. The British had accordingly turned this little island into what Robinson Crusoe would have made if he had lived in the nineteenth century—a commuter suburb to nowhere.

The British are easily seduced by islands. Think of our literature, in which islands are used again and again to demonstrate dramas of ideas: *The Tempest*, *Robinson Crusoe*, *The Coral Island*, Huxley's *Island*, *Lord of the Flies*, etc. For us, the island is a source of wondrous dread—it has a psychology all its own.

Crusoe. Who can make sense of the figure of Crusoe? No one forgets the scene on the island beach where Crusoe first sees the human footprint. The horror of cannibals. And it was an island just like Ross, in its way, with the Jarawa playing cannibal just across the straits. It was Robinson Crusoe who transformed the imperial frontier into a tourist idea, because Crusoe turned the island into an adventure story, a microcosm of Europe and a place that could be remade—all at once.

At the Fortune Resort they had a small library with a

number of enraged ecological texts, a few badly printed local guides, and some "boys' literature," including *Crusoe*
and *The Coral Island*. Since there was nothing else to do between cocktail hour and dawn the following day, I got drunk
on the terrace next to the Jarawa warrior and read the two
books. They made for surprising reading. Defoe's book is
startlingly earnest and grim, for there is nothing romantic
about either Crusoe or his island. It was published in 1704,
before the tropics had become desirable. But Crusoe has all
the traits I see in myself: the longing to get naked, the fastidious disdain bordering on arrogance, the need to "get organized," the utopian desire to transcend the real world. He is
a hedonist and a prig at the same time. He likes the vibe of
coconut palms and beaches, but there is always a tension between the white man and the blacks *who are never there*. A
psychoanalyst would probably delve into the Christian im-
plications of all this, for the Christian template is burned
into every Western secularist. But what of the "cannibals"?
Crusoe's tale is all about them. A Christian must have his
pagan.

When Ross was at its height, every Englishman knew the
Scottish writer R. M. Ballantyne's adventure story *The Coral
Island*. Published in 1857, *The Coral Island* tells the tale of
three plucky English schoolboys, Ralph Rover, Jack, and Pe-
terkin, shipwrecked on a South Seas island paradise. They
immediately claim it as a microcosmic tropical kingdom that
they subdue with all the imperial force that British children
once had at their fingertips. The dialogues are robustly imperial, in the jolliest way:

> "We've got an island all to ourselves. We'll take pos-
> session in the name of the king; we'll go and enter the

service of its black inhabitants. Of course we'll rise, naturally, to the top of affairs. White men always do in savage countries. You shall be king, Jack; Ralph, prime minister, and I shall be—"

"But suppose there are no natives?"

"Then we'll build a charming villa, and plant a lovely garden round it, stuck all full of the most splendiferous tropical flowers, and we'll farm the land, plant, sow, reap, eat, sleep, and be merry."

Then the "savages" arrive. The chapter headings become feverish. "Intercourse with the savages—Cannibalism prevented" and such like. The cannibals arrive by canoe, just as they do in *Robinson Crusoe*. Here is the chief of the anthropophagi:

> He was tattooed from head to foot; and his face, besides being tattooed, was besmeared with red paint, and streaked with white. Altogether, with his yellow turban-like hair, his Herculean black frame, his glittering eyes and white teeth, he seemed the most terrible monster I ever beheld.

I put the book down and watched the same Englishman on his cell phone at the other end of the restaurant, still hunched, still babbling about percentages. The "boys" stood around as they had in a thousand and one colonial bars, arms crossed, subtly sardonic but friendly. I searched their faces for any sign of Jarawa or Onge inheritance, but they were all Indian. This whole place was a descendant of the "charming villa" the British had built on Ross, but the black men who were not there were the invisible shadows that ringed it. The Calibans of Ballantyne's indescribably trite book stretched all the way from British India to British Australia, from Borneo to Papua, from the Andamans to Tahiti. *They* were the Lost World, not the undesert islands they so inconveniently inhabited.

Vinod arrived at five a.m. in a dented Japanese minivan. By now I relished the constant dawn downpour, the compressed scent of datura and mud that hung in the air. We had coffee together on the terrace and discussed our route. His boss had given him all his instructions, including Dr. Apse's police permits for the roadblocks, and had impressed upon him the imperative need to *not* stop on the ATR even for a second. Needless to say, I was determined to sabotage this directive if I could, but for the time being I agreed to it. Vinod was a bit of a player—his cell phone reverberated to constant feminine demands—and he was not really looking forward to this jaunt through the Jarawa lands. Most tourists went to Havelock Island, which was a quick four-hour ferry ride from Port Blair. Why all this driving up to the remote frontier town of Diglipur?

"Nothing to see there." He sighed, as if hoping I would change my mind and take us both to a fine air-conditioned resort on Havelock where there would be plenty of Calcutta girls.

It was a slow ride through the tsunami-wrecked suburbs of Port Blair. The clay road churned in the rain, set between farms submerged like paddies. Road crews assembled in the half-light, rock cutters with puny hammers setting to on piles of boulders. The rain made them dark as iron.

On the far side of the capital, the rain forest begins at

once. Before you know it you are winding through thimbok
trees tall as apartment blocks, feathery with mist, and black
chuglums alive with ants. The jungle is webbed with creepers, like a thick spider's web. After an hour, we approached
the first checkpoint. Here were cultivated fields rammed
against the edge of the forest, a few shacks and a chai stall
piled with fresh chapatis and cans of condensed milk. The
soldiers cowered from the rain, sipping at tiny glass cups. A
large black sign instructed us what to do if we met a Jarawa.
DO NOT GIVE ANY ITEM EATABLE, CLOTHES ETC TO JARAWAS.
DO NOT LET THE JARAWA GET INTO YOUR VEHICLE. SOLITARY
DRIVING RISKS YOUR LIFE AND PROPERTY.

We went to see the policeman with our permit. There was
a "Reporting Room" with a view over the kiwi-green fields.
Yet more bored soldiers sat under the wet palms, watching
the day's first convoy assemble: two buses and us. The papers were stamped and processed through a 1940s type-
writer, the policeman giving us a cool stare. The buses were
occupied by "settlers" making their way to Diglipur and
Ariel Bay, the two northernmost villages of the archipelago.
Over the whole operation lay an atmosphere of lackadaisical
anxiety, of prosaic hysteria in the face of the blacks *who
were not there*. The officer cracked a few jokes about the
Jarawa to rattle us, then looked over the governor's permit.
Not a single outsider had been through here in months, and
dozens of faces peered in through the window at the white
man with his florid permit and his small cigar. When it was
over I went down to the chai stall and got a milky cup to
drink in the rain. It was an anachronistic scene all round,
something out of the '30s, from the travel books I had
grown up on like *Road to Oxiana* and *Journey Without*

Maps, but without the trains of porters, servants, and diplomatic contacts.

The armed guards got on the buses.

The three-vehicle convoy moved off, and Vinod put on some pop music, a band called Dhoom, which means "pleasure" in Hindi. I had the impression that it reassured him amid so much annoyingly pointless nature.

We ate our sandwiches and I stared glumly at hours of passing forest, the forest that really is so boring when it is genuinely wild and is being watched from a car that cannot stop. In the airless heat, immense gurjun trees stood perfectly still above glades of pandanus palms. We passed logging parties with packs of elephants clearing spaces with chains and saws, the foremen packing rifles. On some parts of the road, dirt-poor Bengali farms had sprung up, carving a few paddies out of the jungle, their skinny buffalo tended by boys in dhotis, but soon they seemed suffocating, like model villages built inside caves. There were even occasional repair crews armed with primitive box-shaped steamrollers like armored cars of the Russian Revolution and buckets of pitch. They looked up as we passed, with the haunted eyes of helots.

I asked Vinod if we might pass a Jarawa on the road.

"Very bad guys." He scowled. "Thieving guys."

A subtle tension was now emerging between us and it had something to do with the black men. Was I siding with them against the Indians?

"Vinod," I said, "I'll give you thirty dollars if you stop when we see a Jarawa."

But he shook his head.

"They are watching us from the bus!"

And he was indeed driving right behind the bus, his hand pressed almost continually on the horn. The bus driver was doing the same as the convoy took the endless hairpin turns. With three horns never desisting and the screams of Dhoom, we were a caravan of cacophony. It began to grate on my nerves.

"Vinod, can you get off the horn?"

He looked back with contempt, as if I was the last person to offer advice about this wretched road.

"We drive like this, sir."

"Yes, but off the horn for thirty seconds, can you?"

The head jiggled, and the horn continued droning. It was of course an anti-Jarawa siren. I put in my earplugs. In the middle of a pristine jungle, in earplugs!

At the tip of South Andaman Island you have to take a flat-bottomed ferry across a narrow strait to the small island of Baratang. The forest turns into mangrove swamp studded with frilly orange flowers. The Indians got off their rattling buses decorated with magic eyes and weeping faces of Jesus, under which the words "Jesus Saves!" could be seen again and again. Hinduism seems to have receded before a wrath-ful monotheism more in keeping with frontier realities. The Indians got off their buses and stretched their legs, waiting for the ferry. Their eyes anxiously scanned the forest. They knew they weren't meant to be here, that it wasn't their land. The midday heat scrunched their faces. Where were the funny black men? I walked down to the stone jetties, from where the shrilling cicada song of the jungle projected over flat, glassy waters. I was feeling jarred and irritated, though now suddenly seduced by the mangroves standing above the water on multiple legs, like huge spiders. "Back to the Stone Age"? The ferry was not the *Steinzeit*, but a hundred yards into the forest might be another matter. An end to the comfortable rituals of beds, chairs, and washbasins, an end to TV world and "travel." But there was no way of getting in there.

On a comatose boat, we crossed over to Baratang Island.

On Baratang's northern side yet another ferry takes you over to the much larger but sparsely populated Middle Andaman Island. We drove due north, through lonelier forests. It took the whole day to cross the island, and Vinod and I haggled about the horn and other things. I was growing furious. Each time he honked, I snapped at him.

"Not again, Vinod. I said don't use the horn."

His head jiggled and he put on his gangster shades.

"I am driver," he muttered.

A few miles into Middle Andaman we came to the hideous pit of Rangat, its principal village. Like all the settlements of the Andamans, Rangat boasts little more than a main street of chai stalls, markets offering the cheaper debris of modernity, and the supply stores of impoverished farmers. After Independence in 1947, the Andamans were settled mostly by Bengalis ready to farm and log a formidable wilderness. After the 1973 war in Bangladesh, a flood of Bengali-speaking refugees joined them. I bought some mangoes and wandered around, the object of stares containing neither empathy nor curiosity. Vinod sat on the car and smoked. He waved to a passing pretty girl as if he knew her. I went to have a look at a small lodging called Dream Hotel encrusted into the side of a hill of debris and surrounded by dogs, but Vinod protested that for that night's accommodation he had called ahead to reserve a room in a "four-star" government place ominously called the Hawk's Bill Nest. "Very fine place," he said urgently, staring at me through his shades like a hit man. "You will like it, sir."

The Hawk's Bill Nest lay on a lonely road near the sea, a pale orange wreck that had not seen a visitor in seven months. The gates were rusted, a few letters missing from the sign, and firmly padlocked. A drowsy youth in a loincloth appeared; he stared through the bars for a long time before producing a key.

By now I was beginning to have doubts about this whole enterprise. Into what hotelier nihilism was I now headed? As the gates creaked open, I felt a neocolonial dread.

Government hotels in India are not really hotels; they are casual employment outlets for young men on permanent vacation. A group now roused themselves like sunning puppies disturbed by a bone thrown from a passing car. They looked stunned to see us, raising weary heads from the backgammon board where they had probably been playing for weeks uninterrupted. Alas, there was not a capable woman in sight, which meant that nothing would be done well. This was to be an exclusively male form of torture.

The rooms were named after nearby islands. Mine was named Barren, which was appropriate since there was almost nothing in it. No sheets, a single bar of Ayurvedic soap, and no water in the bathroom. A panel of crude switches looked like something from *Apollo 12*. Eye-killing lamps were fixed to the wall like interrogation instruments, one red, one blue. Would they start flashing alternately in the middle of the night? A maze of concrete passages, stairways, and iron grilles completed the tropical prison look while downstairs a flashy photo mural of a beach dominated the dining room, similarly barren. There was no one there. In the lobby, the boys had gone back to their backgammon board sprinkled with baby powder. They were all thin as poles, with huge rubber flip-flops. When I asked for a towel—just one—they groaned and rolled their eyes, as if being asked for proof of the existence of God. The dialogue unfolded with feverish colonial misery:

"Ah, towel we are not having, sir."

"Sheets?"

The heads jiggled. "Sheets we are not having, sir."

"Where are the sheets?"

"Sheets locked up in kitchen, sir."

"Well, unlock the kitchen."

Heads jiggling. "Not having key, sir."

"Well, get the bloody key, then."

"Cook is having key, sir."

"And where is the cook?"

"Cook in Rangat, sir."

Unable to think of anything else to do, I made one of them ride into Rangat to get some whiskey. He came back with two of the local brands: Antiquity and a noxious brew from Seagram's called Royal Stag. There was a stag on the label. It was a mix of scotch and "carefully selected Indian grain spirits." I went to my room, locked the door, and drank the Antiquity.

Presently, Vinod offered to drive me down to nearby Amakunj Beach. Night was falling and a storm gathering.

A wild forest of Alexandrian laurel comes to Amakunj's edge, dropping whole trees on the beach as driftwood. I waded out into a gray sea. Lightning ripped into the haze and the blue shapes of small barracuda flashed about as if disturbed by the aerial electricity. Stepping into the forest, I ripped off a pandanus fruit and tried to eat it. If the Jarawa ate it, why not me? In the menacing dusk, a few aquamarine fishing boats skimmed past, gunwales dripping with blood, but I must have been invisible—too incredible an apparition?—because no one waved. The pandanus tasted like unripe grapefruit, but I ate it anyway and, sitting on the coral drenched in seeds, I had the first sense of being somewhere on the edge of the world but not really in it.

At midnight, the cook arrived drunk on a moped, full of swaggering malice. He had the storeroom key. His eyes were yellow in the kerosene light and I had to haggle the key out of him. We went to the storeroom and he snatched out a towel and a sheet.

"Inventory!" he cried, by way of explaining something.

I went up to Barren and took my Royal Stag onto the balcony, overlooking a strangely autumnal-looking sea. I felt morose, belligerent. I began drinking heavily. A blood moon emerged through tamarinds; the gurjuns creaked like a ship's rigging. An hour later the electricity went off, never to return. On the road, I saw shadows moving about like disoriented smugglers. I stayed awake until four, when we were due to move off again, and when the dawn tea arrived with a plate of wet biscuits, an ant crawled up from the biscuit onto my lips and bit me in the eye. Within an hour, I looked like Quasimodo. The boys were spooked. Vinod smiled cruelly, and in Rangat we stopped to get some antiseptic ointment.

The day's drive was exhausting. At the tip of Middle Andaman lies the torpid flyspeck of Mayabunder, its bluffs
looking out to a low horizon of intense greenness—the
empty jungles of North Andaman.

On the bluffs stood a government hotel and restaurant,
to which Vinod took me because it was "on the itinerary."
Whose itinerary? I wondered. There was a spectacular
gazebo built right on the water at the bottom of a dizzying
flight of steps. I labored down to get close to the sea's cool
and to watch the waves smashing on the rocks. After forty
minutes, a scowling waiter appeared, clearly annoyed at
having been obliged to make the same trip down. He had a
Salvador Dalí mustache and polished shoes.

"Drinks cannot be here, sir. Please, upstairs."

And he ushered me out of the gazebo and back up the
four hundred steps. There was another gazebo up on the
cliff with beautiful views, but the shade shook his head
again. No, that gazebo was "closed" as well. Visitors had to
eat *indoors*.

"Why?"

"It is rules."

Perhaps it was the eye. He was looking fearfully at it.

"An ant bit me," I said. But his nod was doubtful.

The dining room inside was suffocating but decked out in
High Alpine style. Perforated lace curtains, pine chairs, and
exhortational wall pictures of excessive surreality, mostly to
do with Switzerland and snow. Under one view of a high ski
slope was what looked like a slogan for Viagra: "Harder the
rise, happier the taste!" Vinod went off to eat by himself,

and I was left alone with the fried fish and dal. A youth snored under the washbasin, as if in the grip of a lunchtime nightmare. What was I to think of this mad setting? Obviously the hotel was empty, and who the hell ever came to Mayabunder? One is so used to the infrastructure of mass convenience, to collective conviviality and ease, that as soon as one drops out of this system a sense of paranoia comes quickly. I felt that I was inside some sort of totalitarian contraption designed to make me feel as if I was on holiday.

I went over to Vinod's table and rudely told him that for the next leg of the journey he was to drive a little faster and keep off the horn. In reply, he laughed at my bloated golf ball eye.

"Do you always come to this dump on your tour?"

He nodded sadly. The Indian families liked it.

"You do not like, sir?"

I was beginning to feel that Vinod was playing me for a sucker. I was always being rushed along, even when there was obviously no need whatsoever to rush. We had left at an ungodly hour so that we could catch the ferry on time in Mayabunder, but now it turned out that there was no ferry leaving yet, that in fact there was no ferry at all: we would be walking across a bridge to North Andaman, a bridge that had been damaged by the tsunami and could not be crossed in a vehicle. A different car would therefore be waiting for us on the other side. That car wouldn't be there for another four hours, however. He shrugged. That was why we were in the alpine restaurant.

A journey is never a simple thing. The hitches and the boredom, the missed connections and the empty hours are the price that must be paid for leaving one's real life and en-

tering an unreal one. On the other hand, this temporary unreal life has its advantages. You have nothing to think about
except the logistics of the journey itself, in all their madden-
ing detail and stupidity. With time even these details take on
a poetic urgency. How far is it to the bridge? Is the car waiting on the far side of said bridge? It is only when you are
thoroughly submerged in such questions that you begin to
become *unconscious*.

On the way to the bridge we stopped at a beach and ate
some mangoes. While I stripped off and plunged into the
water, Vinod remained impeccably dressed and watched me
from the car, eating his mango with a penknife. Everything I
did seemed to be in contrast to him, in antagonism to him,
though I couldn't have said why. Between here and the
bridge, however, he didn't use the horn once. We got out at
the checkpoint and hired two porters to carry our bags to
the far side. The bridge, it turned out, had suffered a three-
inch dislocation during the earthquake and couldn't be re-
paired. A gang of men rolled oil drums across with us, and
on the far side a drunk Karen with penis exposed insulted us
all in broken Hindi. The water was black, slow moving. Our
new car was waiting in the shade of the trees.

The anthropologist Bronislaw Malinowski, who roamed the
South Seas a century ago just before the age of Margaret
Mead and Lévi-Strauss, has described the ecstasy of being
immersed in primitivity, an emotion that we can feel less and
less. There are moments, he wrote, "when you merge with
objective reality—pure nirvana."

When Paul Gauguin was on Tahiti in the 1890s, he made

a valiant try at understanding Tahitian culture. But ultimately that wasn't why he was there. He was there to learn
how to take off his clothes. In his little book *Noa Noa*, we
have an account of what could be called Crusoe Syndrome:

> My body, constantly nude, no longer suffers from the
> sun.
> Civilization is falling away from me little by little.
> I am beginning to think simply, to feel only very lit-
> tle hatred for my neighbor—rather, to love him.
> All the joys—animal and human—of a free life are
> mine. I have escaped everything that is artificial, con-
> ventional, customary. I am entering into the truth,
> into nature. Having the certitude of a succession of
> days like this present one, equally free and beautiful,
> peace descends upon me. I develop normally and no
> longer occupy myself with useless vanities.

As we drove through the North Andaman jungles, I
thought about the scene where Gauguin goes into the forest
to chop down rosewood trees with his Tahitian friend,
Totefa. In a fit of madness, he starts lashing out at all the
trees while his ax sings to him, "Destroy in thee all love of
the self!" It's a crazy scene and it ends with a primitivist cry:

> Yes, wholly destroyed, finished, dead, is from now on
> the old civilization within me. I was re-born—

But that "old civilization" obsessed Gauguin much more
than the real Tahiti. How could it not have? Escapism is always an escape from something that dominates you. At the

beginning of *Noa Noa*, Gauguin quotes Baudelaire: *"Dites, qu'avez-vous vu?"* Tell me what you have seen. But Gauguin is not telling us what he has seen; he is not recording the decaying colony in all its picturesque complexity. He is describing himself in all his picturesque complexity. No wonder his Tahiti has inspired so many tourist decors. It was all about the "I."

I stared blankly at my own forest, unable to feel a way into it. No one could tell me what its native name was. Vinod began using the horn again; I leaned forward and shouted at him not to.

"But it is curvy," he protested.

I said there were no Jarawa here. We had not seen even one, much to my chagrin, and he was using the horn to scare off the Jarawa that I wanted to see.

"Jarawa," he muttered, and blew out his cheeks. Was this a safari looking for humans? These forests were empty, anyway, they were lost in a wide sea. The Jarawa had left it a long time ago.

Four hours later, we were in Diglipur. It's a rough-and-tumble country town, all heat and dirt. Around a psychedelically colored temple, a hysterical political meeting was taking place. "Vote for Mr. Bakhta!"

A few miles beyond Diglipur, Ariel Bay must be the most remote village in India. The sea looms up, islands appear in the distance, flashing their sands. Nipa palms shade small houses embedded within rose gardens and pinanga fences. An archaic emotion floods through you.

It is the original British settlement on the Andamans, but

nothing of the former overlords remains. The bay is filled with sunken boats hit by the tsunami, their funnels and bows rising from the water at rakish angles, with logs and floating debris that will never be cleared away. There's one street, open to the fields.

On the far side of the village, the road becomes a narrow track scratched between paddies. Children stand by it like small copper statues, motionless, their eyes wide with amazement. Where this road collides with the rain forest around Saddle Peak, the tallest peak in the Andamans, the Turtle Resort looms up on a hillock of its own, as if guarding that road's end. It is owned by the same management as the Hawk's Bill Nest, that is, the Republic of India.

Labyrinthine and stark, the hotel seems to have sunk into the vegetative life of the forest; thousands of insects purr in its boarded-up corridors. But a genial cook called Mishtry greeted us and promised to open the padlocks of the pantry and find us pillows. The room was decayed. A large picture of the historic Cellular Jail in Port Blair hung between two nightclub lamps, this time one yellow, one red. All the rooms were padlocked. Soon after arriving, however, there was a frantic knocking at my door. Outside, in the dusk, a tall silver-haired man stood in slippers and dhoti. A huge hand slipped desperately into mine, and before I knew it I was locked in a frantic embrace with "Mike." Mike owned a thing called the Coconut Resort across the road.

"You come my place," he whispered, bending closer, "we are having no visitors, my place much better. Promise? Please, sir! Coming visit and having tea with me tonight!"

He clenched me with both hands. The eyes were wild.

"Coconut Resort, sir!"

The dining room was brightly lit, eight fans whirring, but

the boys slept in a torpor by the reception desk. The sea roared close by. Mishtry apologized for the lack of amenities. But were there towels at least?

"Towels we are not having."

The head jiggling began. Bread?

"Bread we are not having."

"Butter," I tried.

"Butter we are not having."

Running water? The head bobbed. "Not having."

"Is it locked up?"

"Not having key, sir."

Later, lying in my room, I turned on a baroque air-conditioning unit attached by a cable to the wall. There was nothing, but they had air-conditioning at least. Raising the bottle of Antiquity to my lips, I felt a sudden triumph—the triumph one feels in enduring entirely irrational obstacles and adversities that should never have been there in the first place. "I've got fuck all here, but there's a cool breeze from the air conditioner and a bottle of ersatz scotch at the end of the world! Not bad!"

Then, with a shuddering moan, the power went off.

At once the heat returned. I struggled onto the balcony and looked down at a garden plunged in darkness. Mishtry was down there, looking up plaintively from amid a herd of long-horned cows, his face faintly picked out by a sliver of moon. He jiggled his head. The cows jostled around him.

"Power we are not having, sir."

For the next few days I hired local fishing boats and roamed around the empty islands scattered around the waters off Ariel Bay like miniature versions of the Coral Island.

The biggest of these is called Smith and Ross—it is actually two islands joined by a sandbar that is exposed at low tide. A boat called *The Shark* goes there in the morning after the rain has stopped. Fishermen sometimes go over with the three Independence War veterans who live there, bone-thin men with hard, bitter faces, hauling lines tied to coral chunks and oyster shells for knives. It is a dreamy voyage; the climate is volatile, constantly electrified. There is a vaporous tension in the air—rainbows, mists, mirages. It is a virginal panorama, so unmanipulated that you immediately doubt its veracity. The islands look like optical illusions and then, with a dull start, you realize that what they really look like are brochure images. Sitting in the waterlogged boat I felt like a prospector searching out new locales for the Four Seasons. All this talk of the Andamans being the next Maldives or Seychelles had only reminded me how much I loathe the Maldives and the Seychelles, classic Wherevers that had gladly accommodated the utopian fantasies of their clientele. But then the Maldives had indeed looked just like this prior to 1972, when twelve Italian writers had been invited to the islands by the international investor George Corbin. The gates were opened; resorts were built using the precious coral that kept the Maldives afloat.

Many writers have called the pre-1972 Maldives a utopian paradise. Thurston Clarke, in *Searching for Paradise*, called it "positively Atlantan," an Atlantis that is waiting to be sunk. After scheduled jet service began, 42,000 tourists in 1980 quickly became 400,000 by the year 2000. Male, the Maldives capital, was turned from a "dazzling white city of coral paths and houses smothered in orchids" into a replica of Honolulu. Before, the sultan owned the only car and people got around on bicycles and sailboats. Paradise! Afterward, the traffic jam and the concrete sky-scraper, the brand resort hotel and the parking lot. The same thing would happen to Port Blair, or even to Ariel Bay. To which the Indians always sighed coolly, saying, "But they are already shit holes, sir."

The Shark drifted into the shallows, a crossbar anchor was thrown, and we waded ashore, the old man carrying his wife on his shoulders. As soon as they were on land, the old couple walked off into the jungle without saying a word, and I was left on the sandbar.

Inside the jungle, the trees were so high that the ground was almost dark, though there rose from it spectral spear-shaped white blooms as tightly rolled as cigars. Clusters of creamy rambai flowers and vanilla orchids burst out on the mossy slopes farther in. As I climbed upward, on hands and knees now on slippery alga, I could hear my heart pounding and I caught myself preparing for Papua, for an Asian forest that would be like this, only worse. But, more than that, I could not decipher it or eke a meaning from it.

"If modern wanderers are to repeat the thrills which early travelers experienced," Margaret Mead wrote from Samoa in 1925, "they will have to cultivate the much neglected senses of taste and smell." And this is what the jungle gives back to you. "The movies and the phonograph have effectu-ally eliminated the other two senses and touch doesn't seem to have much of a role here." I had never thought about it before, but it is likely that the great diaspora of Western travel is a blind search to rediscover the senses. Mead admits it openly. The smell on Smith was frangipani, rotting orchid, seaweed from the drying rock pools permanently exposed by the tsunami, just as on Samoa it was slightly fermented over-ripe bananas, an odor that was "like that of bee-stung grapes." I had never been in a jungle before, just as Mead had never been on a *malaga*, a Samoan "journey" to visit remote markets, and I found that those two senses—taste and smell—suddenly stirred as Mead had suggested. It's as if acids and oils on the air are naturally obvious to the human nose and tongue; you can suddenly "taste" your surroundings. The sensual world reappears, as if it had been hidden behind a wall.

On the long drive back to Port Blair, the tensions between Vinod and me continued to smolder around the question of the Jarawa. Quite unexpectedly, on a lonely stretch of road in the forest, we passed a group of thatch huts sunk in the sunless interior. They flashed by, dark gold in the shadow. But however startling this apparition, it was not quite as startling as the semielegant young Indian man standing on the hard shoulder by a motorbike, smoking a cigarette. The huts were obviously a Jarawa camp and I asked Vinod to slow down.

"Policeman!" he cried, and he hit the gas pedal hysterically.

I touched his shoulder brusquely. "Stop right now!"

He refused and the head jiggling began. "Not stopping, sir!"

Was it an excessive respect for authority or a tedium that could not admit itself, an impatience to get back to the bright lights of Port Blair? We almost came to blows, or severe words at least, but in the end I had to let it go. At the

Baratang ferry, however, I unexpectedly found the motorcy-
clist again. He was reclining on a wall with a pretty Bengali
girl in an outlandish pink sari, and far from being a cop, he
was one Dr. Pronob Kumar Sircar, M.A., M.Phil., Ph.D., research investigator with an organization concerned with the
Jarawa known by the incredible name of Andaman Adim
Janjati Vikas Samiti. In other words, a scholar assigned to
look after "tribal matters" on the Trunk Road.

Pronob spoke fluent Jarawa and quietly followed the
buses on his motorbike. He was bashfully delighted to meet
a foreigner, though it was not at all clear what he was doing
there. Was it true, I asked, that he was following us to make
sure we didn't break the rules?

"Oh yes, certainly." But he laughed with great charm. "I
am undercover!"

I saw that Vinod was glaring at us.

"Is it true," I asked, as urbanely as I could, "that one
cannot talk to a Jarawa?"

"Perfectly true. But would you like to talk to one?"

"If it could be arranged."

"No big deal. There are some over here. Come."

He motioned toward a miserable hut by the road shaded
by a padauk tree, where a gang of Indian soldiers had gathered. From the nudges and giggles I surmised the presence of
aborigines. On the way over, Pronob gave me a quick speech
about the Jarawa.

The Bengalis were teaching the Jarawa a lot of bad
things: obscene slang, tobacco smoking, and so forth. Contact had been calamitous for them. Paradoxically, however,
little is known about the Jarawa. They speak a language totally unrelated to any language group in India or even Asia.

Recent DNA tests on them by teams at the University of Hy-derabad have suggested that they are an incredibly rare group of genetic Africans who migrated to the Andamans via India seventy thousand years ago. Friendly contact was made with them only in 1974. Since 1998, they have come more frequently into settler areas, but for the Burmese, whom they know as poachers, whom they call *bema*, they keep their ancient hatred—every Jarawa carries an arrow specially set aside for killing *bema*. The arrow itself has a special name.

The Jarawa make their living from both the forest and the sea. Their love of seafood can be gleaned in their word for sea—*nappo daang daang incho*, "water where fish thrash about." They make beautiful woven baskets and large fiber belts that serve as body armor. To make arrowheads, they trade tin and iron from the Bengalis and flatten it out with stones into superb blades. Families are patriarchal; men hunt while women gather and fish. Despite their low numbers, anthropologists are surprised to find that no incest exists among them. And yet they are all closely connected through kinship.

Pronob was as nattily dressed as the Jarawa. I couldn't quite figure out what his job actually was—a mix of forest ranger, informal policeman, and tribal counselor?

There were police inside the hut, fingering ancient rifles. Pronob bargained with them to let us in. And there on a mis-erable wooden cot lay a tiny black man wearing a necklace of dried leaves. He lay as if ill—the Jarawa often drift into posts in search of medication—but in one hand he waved a short arrow with a ferocious metal head. *"Paatov."* He smiled. Arrow. Then: *"Thaahoodintaavpaatov."* Arrow for killing Burmese! Everyone laughed. Opposite him sat a beautiful boy so delicately and finely drawn that I mistook him for a naked girl. His chest was painted with red clay, and he wore bright red wool armbands. His cheeks were whitened with ash. The man on the bed reached up and shook my hand, handing me the arrow to feel. The policemen laughed and he laughed with them—but he was an animal trapped among keepers. He asked for his arrow back and took my hand again, rolling it over in his and murmuring to me.

"He say he have tummy ache," Pronob translated. "But he happy to see such big man here."

I walked over to the boy and held out my hand. But the reaction from him was exactly the opposite. He abruptly recoiled his shoulder away from me and grimaced. The large white hand seemed grotesque to him, untouchable. His left hand fingered a large bow laid flat on the cot.

Pronob translated again: "I cannot touch you. Don't know what you are."

It's rare that you meet another person who cannot make up his mind whether you are human or not. The fear flashing across the eyes—mixed with a slight disdain—was deliciously strange. As was the paranoia of the Indians around them. What were they so afraid of? In a moment, I was forcibly whisked away.

Two hours later, black bodies appeared on silent feet, slipping out of the jungle like inquisitive birds.

Now, they were a stranger sight. One was dressed like any Brooklyn rapper, though he carried a thickset bow and yellow clay was smeared around his eyes. His name was Pu, and he asked me in broken Hindi if I wanted to buy his bow.

Before I could accept, the Indians hustled him away to an abandoned house nearby, where the other Jarawa seemed to be congregating. Others milled around the buses. A tiny boy with a baby strapped to his back stopped in front of one bus's fender and suddenly ran his fingers, then his cheek, against the still-warm engine grille. Two tall warriors loped by with spears, their chests and faces smeared with geometrically patterned red clay. Wild grass was draped around their necks, and they wore the Jarawa's characteristic bright red wool armbands. Strings of pink beads hung on their hips. They glared at us and at the Bengalis. The ripple of apprehension was palpable and the Bengali girls cowered. Vinod tried to hurry me away. "Very violent guys, sir!" But I lingered and our eyes met. What I saw, however, was not a pristine "savage" but a half-broken, scavenging forest dweller attuned to the tourist glee of passing Indians. The Jarawa were already canny in the ways of *eenen*.

One of them came up to me slyly and thrust out an ash-caked hand. He said something in rapid Jarawa that was clearly meant for the two of us, since it was evident that my skin and height had surprised him, amazed him even. But of course there was no way I could decipher the words. He came closer for a second, before the Indian soldiers moved toward him, and I thought that his hand darted forward to brush my chest. A blessing or a curse? In that moment, moreover, I realized that it was not I visiting him, but he visiting me. I was the curious, exotic "wild man" standing in the rain in my strange pink shirt and bizarre-looking hat. He was as much a tourist as I was. He therefore smiled, and there was a sparklingly cruel look in his eyes. It could have been regret that he didn't have a camera.

Vinod, of course, was furious.

"Very bad guys, these ones. And you were talking to a policeman!"

We argued about it in the car as we headed south.

"I thought they were rather pitiful," I said flatly.

"You not knowing these guys, boss. Pretty tough!"

But I soon spotted the bow he had bought from Pu when I wasn't looking. On the road, he loosened up and admitted that he often took pictures of them with his cell phone and showed them to his girlfriend. He also had a fine collection of Jarawa bows and arrows in his flat. They were all rogues together, in a sense. Everyone took pictures of them except, of course, foreigners.

"Vinod, you are a complete fraud." I laughed.

"Ah, you also, sir!"

"Fair enough. Sell me that bow, though?"

"No, no, sir. Bow is for girlfriend."

By the time I got back to the Fortune Resort, my eye had swollen to the size of a small tangerine. As I walked into Charles Correa's lobby, which now seemed elegant with its Bruckner symphonics and fish tanks, there was a gasp from the staff followed by merriment. It is socially acceptable, it seems, to laugh at a man's eye if it has been bitten by a venomous *myrmex*. I ordered room service, Antiquity on the rocks, and collapsed onto the bed with a fever, smothering the eye with an ointment from reception. Thank God, I kept thinking, I am flying to Bangkok tomorrow morning. For I had planned Bangkok as a medical stopover as much as anything, a place to avail myself of cheap malaria medications, some dental work, and perhaps some other more esoteric preparations for mind and soul before the far more radical leap into Papua. The weaknesses and flaws had already been exposed by the Andamans. Large cracks had appeared inside me, the signs of imminent breakup. I was drinking heavily; the heat was unhinging me. I kept thinking of the colonial class in their stand-fall collars and three-piece suits. How stoic it seemed, beyond reason. Of course, in most countries they had their cooler hill stations, but not here. I turned on the TV and watched the Calcutta stations as night fell and the fishing boats lit up across the bay. My hand was shaking. I could not put two thoughts together; all desire had seeped away. A purification? A breakdown of the corpuscles, the molecules, the atoms? I took two Ambiens, but the sea kept me awake. The sea always keeps me awake. Fucking nature, I thought. What I needed now was two weeks in Hedonopolis.

HEDONOPOLIS

In the lobby of Thailand's most august hotel, the house string quartet had just struck up "The Blue Danube." The high notes were a halftone out of tune and nobody was dancing, but the lobby still brimmed with the fever mood of Hedonopolis, the world's pleasure capital. I slumped in one of the lobby chairs and watched the Japanese executive groups and the *farang* businessmen with their Bangkok girls flirting to the sound of "The Blue Danube" under huge bell-like lanterns. (The term *farang* derives from *français*. The French were the first Europeans that the Thais encountered, in the seventeenth century—and so all Western foreigners are still called *farangs*, a word by turns neutral and ominous.) The Oriental has something maniacal about it—circular fountains of unreal flowers, ornamental elephants, ubiquitous mirrors. Here is the apex of the nation's tourist sector, the nub of it all. Thai film stars swept in on their way to the Normandie restaurant. A nervous *farang* in a pinstripe suit with a six-foot ladyboy bar girl picked their way slyly toward the elevators. I looked down at the suede shoes I had just laced up in the Somerset Maugham Suite, where I was lodged with a carved four-poster and a satyric portrait of the old boy. As the couple were politely intercepted—the Oriental is one of the rare Bangkok hotels that cannot bring themselves to condone *amour entre hommes*, despite its adulation of Somerset—I had a premonition that if I converted to Buddhism it was possible that in the future I would be reincarnated as a *kathoey*, a ladyboy; or else as an eel, I could not decide which. I looked carefully at the shoes—they looked hedonistic after the forests of the Andamans. The couple sat right next to me, and the ladyboy noticed them as well. She shot me a brilliant smile and a shoe compliment. "You very bad man!"

In his book *Very Thai*, Philip Cornwel-Smith offers the opinion that "the country probably has no more homosexuals than any other . . . but . . . the Thai physique, smooth skin, love of beauty, refined culture and tolerance enables more of them to flower." When they have been sex-changed, they are often a hallucination. They are "sirens of street culture since ancient times." Thais also call them *faa chamloeng*, "angels in disguise."

There is no society on earth more tolerant of the sexual drive than Thailand. Especially delicious is the Thai idea of sex as a series of gradated moods, each of which has its name: *len pheuan*, "playing with a friend" (for girls), *len sawaad*, "playing at love," and so on. And so there is also *seua bai*, "bisexual tiger." (Around two thousand people surgically change their sex in Thailand every year.) Like the Venice of the Grand Tour, Bangkok has made itself a center of world tourism, the seventh most visited city on the planet and rising, and it has done this by imitating Venice's openness to the sex drive. No other city admits human nature as it really is, without trying to pretend otherwise. For Buddhists, this is simple; for everyone else it appears to be impossible. Few scholars of intercultural relations can say why.

I looked down at the shoes again. Suede? But in Hedonopolis they seemed appropriate. The ladyboy and client moved on, and there was a reprise of "The Blue Danube." Strangely enough, I wanted to dance. My hand had stopped shaking and I was drinking nothing more than a shandy— glorious how Thailand has all the British drinks—along with a plate of Thai spiced peanuts. It was now my sixth hour in the metropolis and the Jarawa already seemed a distant phenomenon, let alone a distant memory. I looked up and found a small, incredibly pretty girl sitting next to me, with a hideous pink hair clip shaped like a predatory butterfly. The gaze was not innocent, nor was it venal. It was uninnocently unvenal. She put her hands together—a *wai*—and uttered the obligatory *sawadee ka*. As any visitor knows, it is almost alarmingly easy to meet Thais who are bent on meeting you. There is nowhere to run. And why would you run? Her name, she said, was Lek.

In the ballroom atmosphere of the Oriental lobby, lit by *King and I* chandeliers, I felt like an English sailor on a Samoan beach. Sailing from island to island, aimlessly and venally, greeted by Lek, who wanted money, amusement, kicks, a shot at love, a break from the street. It is the femininity that had seduced the probably bisexual Margaret Mead. The Samoan girls are well described in the literature, which is not to say they have been described as they are: honey skinned, petite, incapable of our *pudeur*, lasciviously merry, subtly sly, etc. And it struck me that in some ways Bangkok has become not just our Venice but also our Samoa, our landlocked metropolitan Polynesia. It is Samoa, if you like, reinvented as a twenty-first-century *Blade Runner* city.

Lek was far more aware of this than I could be. She was dressed like any five o'clock commuter on the Skytrain. On the surface, Thais are prim, modest, and reserved. But they accept the divergence of appearance and actual behavior. Thais in particular separate gender, which is a public artifact to be kept *riab roi* (proper), and sexuality, which remains undiscussed and *therefore* unrestrained. Lek suggested a drink at the Bamboo Bar, where she could smoke a cigar, and walking beside me the casual bellhop observer was not to know that she was not my travel agent. If my Thai had been better, however, I would have known that *lek* means "small," and in a country of diminutive women a woman has to be absolutely tiny to earn that nickname. When we stood, she came up to my hip. She giggled. Soon, she was laughing uncontrollably. The bellhops laughed as well. In my suede shoes I had become a six-foot-five-inch-tall Jacques Tati, lacking only a raincoat and a pipe—awkward, gangling, as un-Thai as a man can be. But Thai women are also bold. She demanded a Cuban cigar at the bar. "You German rich man lawyer," she said, stroking my leg.

"No," I replied. "Me broke English travel writer."

"Trarer?" She lit the cigar, and suddenly empathetic deliciousness broke out on all sides. "What is?"

"Like chess game. Useless."

"You bad man!"

Opened in 1876, the Oriental is one of the oldest hotels in Asia. Like the Raffles Hotel in Singapore, it made its fortune from the opening of the Suez Canal, through which companies like the East Asiatic Company began taking boatloads of European tourists hungry for "the East." It was a "grand hotel," a new concept, and it was built inside a city with no roads, no hotels, no restaurants, and no *farangs*. It was King Chulalongkorn, crowned in 1868, who opened Bangkok to the West, and the grand hotel was his instrument.

The grand hotel was conceived as a self-contained world which, for the first time, combined all aspects of travel: accommodation, catering, laundry, exchange services, telephone operators, sports, and social facilities. It was usually executed in buff white Neoclassical style—the bland operational style of British colonial buildings that reassured the clientele. Overbearing Western luxury was planted directly in the middle of overbearing Eastern poverty, and the contrast was not avoided; it was even played up. The European tourist of 1870 was hyperconscious of being an imperial creature, though the Kingdom of Siam was not a colony in any way. The grand hotel was his peaceful gunship and it had to loom impassively over the natives. In the insular East of that century, the culture shock must have been immense.

With its opera soirees and crystal chandeliers, the Oriental rose from the banks of the Chao Phraya like an imperial fata morgana, quickly seducing the Thai aristocracy and becoming a prestigious address in the social calendar. "When a European colonist had the courage to build this, the first great hotel," wrote Professor Maxwell Sommerville, visiting the Oriental in 1897, "all classes of Siamese opened their eyes with wonder. Somebody was fashioning an ark in their midst." He reported that stupefied Thais visiting the Oriental often remarked *"Tam jai, tam jai,"* or "Please yourself, please yourself!"

The same story was repeated all over Asia. Planted along

the shipping routes, the grand hotels became oases of alien luxury visited by the hodgepodge elites of Europe. The Galle Face in Colombo, the E & O Hotel in Penang, the Hotel de l'Europe and the Adelphi in Singapore, the Hotel des Indes in Jakarta, the Bela Vista in Macao, the Hong Kong Hotel, the Raffles chain in Cambodia and Singapore: they were all arks. Almost every one of them, if it is still in operation, will have a Somerset Maugham Suite and a Colonial Bar with rattan furniture. At the Oriental, Noël Coward loved "the livery-coloured water" seen from the back terrace at cocktail hour. Joseph Conrad, who took over a ship called the *Otago* here in 1888, was also a frequenter of the bar—hence there is also a Joseph Conrad Suite upstairs in the Authors' Wing.

The Oriental cultivates a very deliberate literary air, with all the trappings and decors of literariness: cane chairs, potted palms, high tea, a library of snoozy clocks and glass book cabinets. The library walls are crammed with portraits of the usual suspects. Evelyn Waugh, Pierre Loti, Somerset. I noticed, however, the lugubrious addition of Jeffrey Archer, labeled the Baron Archer of Weston-super-Mare (as yet, no Jeffrey Archer Suite). Inside the Somerset Maugham Suite, the theme continues as the Great Man's Boudoir, with red velvet walls and gilded stags. I was allocated a butler dressed in gray silk with the marvelous name of Thaworn Champihom.

From the Authors' Wing parlor—the Japanese ladies play cards there all day—an underground passage runs to the lobby. The boutiques are wherevery: Burberry, Lotus Arts de Vivre, Cabochon jewelers, Pink Poodle. There is a small waterfall and a pebbled stream.

I thought of a strange article I'd read in the Thai Airways

brochure coming over from Calcutta, about a concept called "unseen Thainess." It was, our article said, an "invisible product" that emanated from tradition, culture, and "a belief in sacred things." Marketers have long advised the Thai tourist industry that although Thailand produces few recognizable consumer brands, the country is itself one. Marl Lindstrom, the Swedish expert on branding, has even said that the "Buddhist belief system" is part of the brand that consumers use when they visit Thailand as tourists.

Thailand is indeed an astonishingly successful "country brand" that sells itself as such. And the Thai idea of beauty was surely contained in both the aforementioned unseen quality and the savvy required to put this quality to use.

From the first day, I had a medical agenda for Bangkok. I lay all day in bed with brochures of clinics, hospitals, and spas costing a fraction of what they would in the United States or Europe.

It wasn't only my teeth that I could at long last repair in preparation for the life-threatening conditions of the Papuan hinterland. It was also my skin, my kidneys, my endocrine system, my failing eyes, my nails, my hair, my feet, my intestines, my bones, my spleen, and, if I liked, my soul. Repair of the last item seemed to be thrown in more or less free with any of the others, especially if it was combined with yoga. I began to feel restless, pacing up and down with a brochure for "skin perfection" or "muscle toning" and wondering if I was really looking more exhausted than I might *if I only laid out the cash.* Many of the clinics offered things called "cosmeceuticals." On Sukhumvit Soi 1, all the cosmetic surgery

outfits offered steep walk-in discounts. Simple curiosity began to tip me over toward the idea of intervention, experi-
mentation. For the medical tourist is the victim of an
incessant appeal to his or her own curiosity—you want to
find out about your own health, to delve deeper into yourself. In other words, you become the object of your own
curiosity.

I nevertheless attempted the older-fashioned tourist ex-
cursions. Wat Po and the river temples, the floating markets,
the Jim Thompson House. I took the river taxi down to Wat
Po and, with a digital camera, wandered around the glitzy
enameled temples with an ever-darkening sentiment of ignorant disorientation. Wat Po is a Spectacle. But what does it
mean? I sat in the temple café and read some of the guidebooks on Buddhism, like all the other tourists. It was just
like the Chinese tourists who sit in the park behind Notre-
Dame in Paris trying with evident boredom to fathom something about the absurdities of Catholic theology. Confronted
with a part of the global Spectacle, you seek to unravel its
code, though seldom with much success. Meanwhile, you
are hounded on all sides by demented touts who show you
no mercy as you try to arrive and depart from the Spectacle
with dignity. They run after you holding up chits of paper
that look like used lottery tickets, crying, "You wa' temple,
water taxi, nice girl shag?" An afternoon at Wat Po was
enough. Returning to the Oriental, I vowed never to visit another temple again—for, on second thought, the same energy
could be used to shop around for blood-rejuvenation packages.

Quite rapidly, therefore, I lost interest in the historical
area around the river, the area subtending to the Oriental,

and turned to Sukhumvit Road, the great artery that slices through Bangkok and around which is encrusted most of its *farang* entertainment and business. Sukhumvit is perhaps the greatest urban axial road in the world today in the sheer weight and density of pleasure it offers. Although few tourists realize it, it stretches all the way to the beach city of Pattaya sixty miles southeast of Bangkok. It is here that two great succors of the human body converge—fucking and medicine. Sukhumvit has actually reinvented medicine itself to make it something it has never been in all its short if illustrious history: a pleasure.

Instead of visiting Wat Po and the other marvels of history that Bangkok aka Krung Thep, City of Angels, has to offer, I began to take a morning cab to the congested lower end of Sukhumvit, where there were scores of clinics to shop around in. I collected price lists for acupuncture and water therapies, dental plans and hepatitis and malaria shots. I brought them back to the Oriental, where Thunaworn would pick through them as they lay on the desk in the study. Several times he asked me whether I was an invalid. If I was an invalid, he said, his sister had a remedy for anemia that used a whole rabbit and water buffalo's blood. He was not joking. But I pointed to my teeth and related their sad history of fear and neglect. I had not been to the dentist in eleven years. He wagged his finger and the eye twinkled. "You very bad man! You sad tooth!" And he made a face like a wounded molar, if that is possible.

"I am doing my teeth, Thunaworn. It is why I am in Bangkok. I cannot go to the jungle with a bad tooth. What if I have a dental crisis hundreds of miles from anywhere?"

Thunaworn made another sad face. "You fucked, sir."

On one of these prospective jaunts to Sukhumvit I came across an incredible hospital called Bumrungrad near Soi 3. It's the biggest private hospital in Southeast Asia, servicing nearly a million patients a year from 140 countries, 300,000 of them foreigners. It's a medical supermarket. Hundreds of treatments are gathered under one roof, along with restaurants, shops, galleries, and fringe clinics offering variations on the hospital's scientific treatments, a large part of which are cosmetic. The Cosmetic Surgery unit is one of the busiest in the world, famous for its sex-change operations and discount liposuctions. The hospital offers accommodation just like a hotel, including a Royal Suite and room service. It would probably be a wonderful place to die.

There is no imaginable procedure that is not a tenth the price in Bangkok that it would be in London or New York. The city offers bizarre pseudomedical fusions of East and West that would be illegal in a Western country. Statistics from the Tourism Authority of Thailand show that in 2002 foreigners looking for health care in Thailand grew by thirteen percent over the previous year, with 632,000 foreigners visiting thirty-three private hospitals. One in ten tourists traveled to Thailand specifically for medical treatment, the biggest customers being Bangladeshis, followed by Americans and the British.

Even at Bangkok's international airport, I had noticed that the free city maps handed out at the information booth prominently advertised all the plastic surgery clinics. One such was Bangmod Hospital, which offered breast implants, face-lifts, abdominoplasty, cut-price liposuction, double eyelid surgery, nose implants, laser skin resurfacing, and "sex reassignment surgery." The twelve-member Stock Exchange

of Thailand health-care services index—which includes
health giants like Bangkok Dusit Medical Services and Bumrungrad Hospital—has risen more than 350 percent since
July 2000, three times more than the broader Thai stock
market. Medicine is big business in Thailand—the haphaz-
ard fruit of globalization and outsourcing. It is already legendary for its sex-change procedures. You can book into a
hospital-hotel, order in room service, have your sex
changed, recuperate around the pool for a week, then fly
home with a lasting tan. Cocktails are thrown in free.

The Bangkok Dental Hospital lies on Soi 49 near Sukhumvit
Road. The *soi*, or small streets, in this area of the city are
where the new Thai middle class want to live, and the clinic
is surrounded on all sides by Corbusier-like high-rise apartment complexes fresh with recent paint. Too far to walk
from the main road, the facility is serviced by fleets of taxis
carrying the affluent white families from California and the
Ruhr who come here to have their children's teeth fixed.

It is, as you walk in up the white steps, like an installation from the British TV series *The Prisoner*: a futuristic set
burbling with multilingual voices. A serpentine pool, a small
espresso bar, red and purple seats, an atrium sustained by
flashy metal columns. *Très Hong Kong*, in the words of an
elderly woman who labored in from the street clutching her
jaw. Through high glass windows a tropical garden could be
seen, in which Muslim women in chadors pruned away in
the sunlight. Mickey Mouse faces were plastered over a wall
and the blond children sat obediently in their purple seats
awaiting their ordeals.

The staff of this James Bond contraption were all female, hand-selected one would have said for attributes little associated with the rigors of dentistry. They swept around its airy spaces in white heels and starched hats, and their allure could not by any stretch of the imagination have been accidental. It is curious that the West has not yet understood the potential chemistry of sex and dentistry.

Even the dental X-ray was erotic. My head clasped in the machine's arms, I saw my face reflected in an oblong mirror that revealed how flushed it was as I bit on the little yellow plastic mouthpiece. The assistant saw it too and smiled. The X-ray tube rotated automatically around my head, perhaps revealing to a hidden camera the neural glow of a repressed lust. But surely, I wondered, you cannot feel lust in an X-ray machine? A dental technician came and sat with me inside a functional office. She was as beautiful as all the others. She *wai*'ed and said her *sawadee kap*. Then we looked somberly at the X-rays.

"You no be dentist long time?"

I fear dentists. A sadistic old man pokes around in your mouth and tells you to stop crying. Everything reminds you of hospitals and therefore of death. Not in Thailand. Here, the male edge has been erased from things: delight returns. The fillings and the high-fusion metal crown would require four surgeries spread over a week. The total cost would be $383, anesthetics included. In New York, it had simply been unaffordable, well over $8,000.

The surgery room overlooked a placid suburban house and its garden. Four female technicians entered and *wai*'ed. They said they had been shocked at the number of my cavities; I had been skating on thin ice indeed. They began, and I lapsed into a quiescent contentment, the rubberized hands reminding me of those exquisitely carved carrots made to look like roses that one gets in Chinese restaurants.

It was a stormy day, the palms outside the window tossed about with a dry hiss. Between procedures I was advised not to look in a mirror. Downstairs in the atrium café I drank espresso after espresso, still fascinated by the Muslim women tending the tropical garden. Were Muslim gardeners cheap? There were plenty of Westerners eager to chat, which was to say compare their experiences, prices, and bargains. Most were not in Bangkok simply to do their teeth.

Joel, a systems manager from Oakland (in my notes I wrote, "A little shifty, very bad teeth for an American"): "My girlfriend went to Landmark Plaza yesterday. There's the wildest clinic on the fourth floor. She had a colonic irrigation done. Flushed her out with coffee. I'm going tomorrow."

A blond family listened intently. Colonic irrigation? The wife pulled a face.

"I would do it," her spouse said loudly.

So would I, I thought lazily. It was a vile prospect, but I would do it in Bangkok. The barriers of shame were beautifully lowered in this country. Besides, I had been thinking of something to clean out my digestive system before entering a place—Papua—where the diet would be radically raw and primitive.

"Having your teeth done is bad enough," I offered. "But come to think of it, I haven't been to the doctor in eleven years, either."

"Eleven years?" they cried in unison.

"I never have any money," I protested. "One hundred and forty dollars just to get some flu medication?"

"You can get it here for eight dollars," Joel said, indicating that he and his girlfriend had done just that. "We stock up every year. In California they're trying to ban Sudafed in pharmacies because meth labs use it. So we all have to suffer. We get our meds in Malaysia and here. The only things you can't get over the counter are heart drugs and the more powerful sleeping pills."

After the last filling for the day, I took a cab to the Landmark Plaza, my face puffed up like a football, and had yet more espressos in the ground-floor café that looks out onto the busiest part of Sukhumvit Road. I was thinking over the coffee-irrigation thing. Why not? If I could get the teeth done, why not the intestines as well?

It was raining again, and a thousand transparent umbrellas battled through sidewalks choked with food stalls, whores, multilingual neons, tangled cables, and the dripping vaults of the Skytrain. Everywhere on Sukhumvit, half-finished glass-and-steel towers soar above construction lots. Palms wilt within ever-sprouting clouds of steam. In the monsoon gloom, a gigantic image of a female face rose into the sky, only her left eye illuminated by a suspended construction crew. Blind *wanipok*, street buskers, played through traffic fumes, screaming over electric mandolins. An old Muslim gent in a woolly hat trotted by with two hookers from the nearby Nana Complex on his way to the infamous Grace Hotel on Soi 3. An elephant waddled past with a four-foot minder. Nobody bats an eyelid at such things. Inside, the Landmark was all corporate sleekness, the escalators filled with women in business suits on their way to various air-conditioned offices.

The fourth floor was mostly taken up by a furniture store, its showroom piled with extravagant bridal beds and armoires. Behind this lay the G2B or Green To Balance clinic, a short wall of glass hiding a cramped office. I looked around a little apprehensively. Was it a legitimate clinic? In Bangkok, it would not be an unlikely scenario if G2B turned out to be a brothel. I went in nonetheless and was quickly greeted by an eloquent Indian doctor in a white coat, with the largest earlobes I had ever seen.

"Did you make an appointment?" he said, in a thick German accent. "Dr. Eddy Betterman," he added, shaking the hand. "Ja, come in."

German? It was enough for the word just to float through the mind.

We sat and discussed the treatments that G2B offered.

"Integrated is the coming trend in medicine," Eddy said confidently as I perused the brochure. "Yes, integrated. We are an integrated medicine clinic. Western, Chinese, Thai, psychological. We call it Marvelous Integrated Medicine."

He leaned forward, gulped from a glass of water, and looked very carefully at my skin, my hands, my hair.

"Are you sick and tired?" he asked.

"Sometimes."

"Then what you need is a Person-Centered Diagnosis. Here we do a sophisticated blood analysis to determine what needs to be done. We'll blow up images of your blood and project it onto this TV monitor here."

"I am going to Papua," I said. "And I thought I could get sort of cleaned up here first. Detoxed. I need to be fit."

"Ah, Papua you say? Well, you will need to get your blood *very* clean for that. You will have to get the hepatitis shots, too."

"Can you see if my blood is—ah—strong?"

The prices were very reasonable, I was there, and I had nothing to do for the afternoon, so I signed on for a Live Blood Analysis. Meanwhile, I scoured their brochure. There was Chelation Therapy, an herbal sauna and ozone bath called G2B Steam, Lymphatic Activating, Ultrasound-Herbal Oil Massage, colon cleansing, acupressure, and a "foot spa." There was a one-day cleansing spa with colonic irrigation, which might well be the best option for the following day. But first we had to do the blood. A medical nymph took the sample, murmuring, "Are you pain?" While he smeared it onto a microscope plate, Eddy explained how it was he had come to open a practice in Bangkok.

"I started in India with Ayurvedic. But because of the violence in Sri Lanka I lost a lot of patients, so in 2000 I came to Bangkok and looked around for an alternative site. I saw that a lot of Westerners were traveling to Bangkok to get unconventional treatments, because they are sick of the treatments they are getting back home. Here, they can try something innovative, something new. They can experiment. Bangkok is so unregulated compared to the West. They're a little scared at first, then they get quickly hooked on all the possibilities."

It had been a struggle, Eddy said, to get his *own* idea of treatment. But Eastern intuition could indeed be married to Western technology. You had to know where the fine border between the two lay.

"And now, we have a lot of German equipment. Our colonic irrigator is Canadian. It only uses gravity, very gentle, so there are no unpleasant accidents!"

Laughing in the detached medical way (teeth barely bared), he turned on the monitor attached to the microscope, and there was my blood. Eddy could now see "every crystal" in the blood, its pH level, its "texture." Living in America, it was likely that I ate too much acid food and not enough alkaline. I had blood type O, a type that derived straight from the jungle, thousands of years of fighting elephants, etc., so I needed "a lot of exercise." But all in all, he cried, it was beautiful blood. No crystals, perfectly pure.

"You have a baby's blood! Look at this, nurse. Have you ever seen such nice blood?"

The nurses came over and admired. They wore purple dresses decorated with gold grape cluster motifs, like air stewardesses.

"But you still need to do a colonic irrigation, I'm afraid."

He drew a swift diagram of the colon on a notepad and explained to me how it all worked. The colon was shaped like a serpent; inside its crooks waste collected and produced eventual disorders. Only a radical flush could clear it all out.

"You drink milk?" he suddenly asked. "Well, you cannot. Alcohol? You cannot." We made an appointment for the following morning for the one-day colonic spa option.

Eight a.m. at G2B: the new arrival is wrapped in a tiny kimono and led to a treatment room covered with tourist posters of the Greek island of Mykonos. The technical irrigation team, alas, was three young girls. The machine was labeled Whirlpool and was made in Malaysia, not Canada.

Thai cabaret music on the sound system—a lone piano in a large hall. The girls peeled off my kimono with such delicacy that I hardly noticed its departure. Dr. Eddy stuck his head in for a second and cried, "Internal beauty, remember!" The girls giggled. One of them held a rectal tube. "You lie down now!"

As this appliance was thrust into me, the lead technician asked me what I thought of her two assistants. "They beautiful, no?"

Internal beauty is a difficult concept to grasp, made easier, perhaps, by having beautiful girls ram tubes into your ass. Having three girls ram a tube into your ass turns out to be the easiest thing in the world. You are forced to surrender unconditionally. I looked up at the images of Mykonos. Warm coffee was now flowing into my insides, gently pushed by the Whirlpool machine with the gurgling sound of a hookah. The girls joked around, taking turns holding the tube. A superficial calm descended. The irrigation takes patience and serenity. Gradually, you begin to lose control of your own intestines: it is like a bout of scientifically controlled diarrhea. I began to sweat copiously. "You pain?" they kept asking. "I no pain." Above, the white windmills of Mykonos blazed against blue skies. They had seen much irrigational sodomy, I supposed. The girls then exited the room for a moment, giggling anew, and left me sweating on the gurney with the Whirlpool gurgling and my innards rotating slowly like a man in a jet fighter spinning out of control. When they returned, they pushed the hose in a little farther and I felt hot coffee escaping in a sudden rush. "Oh dear, oh dear," they began crying, and I heard the Thai word for doctor.

It was too late. The gastric Chernobyl was in motion. Suddenly, all hell broke loose. It was as if the entire contents of my insides were being liberated from the straitjacket of shame and a lifetime of overindulgence. There was a gasp from the girls. The inundation was sudden and unstoppable. There was panic. They raced back and forth with paper towels, shrieking in a calm Thai sort of way, and the Whirlpool chugged a little faster, more ominously. The cascade, however, threatened to flood the corridor outside and immediate evacuation was necessary. They apologized and *wai*'ed. "We back soon. No worry."

An hour later, the crisis contained, they took me by the hand to the Ozone Treatment room. One of the nurses was called Elena. She had trained in Rome. In no time we were chattering away in Italian as she opened a wooden contraption with a head-sized hole cut into its upper lid. The ozone treatment lasted an hour and was something like a vertical steam bath, but with the threat of mysterious rays bombarding the skin.

"Oh, I loved Rome," Elena was saying, filing her nails. "All those churches."

Afterward, a massage in a small room with a single bulb that changed from blue to red. A poster on the wall showed a fork of violent lightning and the word "Energy!" Outside, visible through one-way windows, young couples tried out the voluptuous Chinese bridal beds in the furniture showroom. I asked the masseuse what her name was.

"Um," she said, walking on my spine.

"Um, me pain now."

"You no pain. Um no pain. You like energy?"

Dr. Eddy saw me out.

"It's a fine feeling, isn't it? You feel lighter, ten years younger. You should do an irrigation every year."

"I feel strange, Dr. Eddy."

"How is that, sir?"

"I don't know. Aroused."

He laughed nervously, handing me his card for future reference. "Welcome to Bangkok."

To my surprise, I found that it was already night. What else was there to do but walk over to Nana Complex?

On Sukhumvit, leaf-green awnings spread the light of a tropical forest in the middle of the night. Behind them the new but unfinished towers looked like the ruins of an ancient city, if the ancient city happened to be downtown Dayton, Ohio. The American hotel chains dominate the skyline, Hiltons, Marriotts, Sheratons, and Westins, whose opulent lobbies and bars are the city's upmarket social spaces. As in downtown Dayton, there are almost no Americans on the streets; it's an American city with no Americans, American torpor replaced by the lecherous vitality of the Asian metropolis. A cunning mix-and-match carried off with charming insolence.

In the Nana Complex on Soi 2, a sex mall gives you themed experiences: girls in orthopedic strapped boots in the Mandarin; the obvious in Schoolgirl; the northern rice farmers in Rainbow and Rosemary dancing on tables to northern pop, the men virtually lost in a seething stew of female energy. A Thai woman once explained to me, "Up north, they do nothing for six months of the year but party, sleep, and fuck. In Bangkok, they spend their six months off between rice harvests partying, sleeping, and fucking. Except here they get paid to do it." A new law forces the bars to close at two a.m., so the Nana girls disgorge at that hour into the parking lot of the Nana Hotel, which also has its own pickup club next to the ground-floor coffee shop. They sit on the cars eating satay sticks, singing away. Available beauty organizing its own commerce legally. I met a friend and his wife at Mandarin, and we went to eat on the street.

Bangkok has the best street food on earth, but what is striking about this literally movable and archaic feast is that it is always sandwiched between the corporate towers of isolating whereverness. It is a survival of nomadic food-on-the-go amid a static Western urbanism imagined by gloomy architects who could never envisage people down on the streets below enjoying themselves. The Western architect, after all, never considers such things for a second; they are irrelevant. If Thai Buddhists are urged to live in the present moment, savoring the principle of *sanuk*, or "fun," then Bangkok street food is the ultimate proof that they are determined to do so and that nothing—not even the ghastly laws of contemporary "architecture"—can get in the way of *sanuk*'s insidious flow. Thus does improvised food unravel the very premise of the Wherever city, and just in the nick of time. I have often thought that such food, sweeping like a delectable tide of odors and textures on a thousand castors throughout the night, could save even American or European cities from their puritanical and overregulated frigidity. Biting into a stewed pig leg or grilled squid long after midnight on the sidewalk tables of Sukhumvit's little *soi*, you cannot help but reflect that this elemental pleasure would be illegal virtually anywhere in the West. Here almost anything

in the organic world can be skewered on bamboo sticks—
Thais call snack food *khong khlob khio*, something you can
"bite and chew." These glistening sticks seem to line entire
streets under billows of peppered steam: cuttlefish, buffalo
meatballs, squid, shark, shelled eggs, wontons, and probably, in some neighborhoods, grilled crickets. On some streets
you can find vats of boiled flower juice, chrysanthemum,
roselle, and pikul, herbal shots served in plastic bags. For
dessert, Soi 38 is the place; the vendors serve mango and
sticky rice, the mangoes buttery and without fiber, dark gold
in color, and ripe all the way through.

A Bangkok night is roomy and easily improvised, as you
might imagine the nights of Rome in the dolce vita '50s—
charmingly provincial and casually sophisticated at the same
time. There is very little posing or self-consciousness. There
are lounges, garden restaurants, superb hotel bars, clubs,
night markets, places in the *soi* off Silom with cushions
strewn on the sidewalk. We moved to Q Bar, which was
once in Saigon. The Saigon owner, New Yorker David Jacobson, now lives here, having been expelled from Vietnam
under obscure circumstances. Q Bar is two floors of *farang*
men and Thai girls—some professionals, some not. With
his cropped gray hair and loopy glasses, Jacobson looks
like every cliché of a Bangkok expat that you might have
concocted in your mind. On an outside terrace we were
served vodka-infused blueberry Jell-Os by Thai models in
snow-white wigs.

"Ironically, there's an American fear of Bangkok," Jacobson was saying, though not, one assumes, from personal
experience. "The men downstairs are mostly European.
Americans want to go to Hawaii and stay inside a lifeless

fortress. They *think* about a city like this more than they actually come here. Maybe, in a weird way, the sex here threatens them as much as the fear of being blown up by Al Qaeda cells. Suddenly it's available. All the fantasizing and neurosis and sex-obsessed sadomasochistic hassle in America disappear." For Thais, I had heard it said many times, it was like an itch that had to be scratched, not a religious drama with penalties. Was the allure of Bangkok that here hetero men could for a week or so live like gay men? Go out every night and get laid. Prowl, trawl, "get trade." The old could come back to life—old men, anyway.

Behind us, an ancient American sat haggling with five girls, a negotiation carried on in passive-aggressive undertones and sudden hand gestures.

"Six?" the old codger hissed. "Six?"

The girls smiled like small toy Buddhas. "You no good man, you no wa' shag?"

Here money was openly used as a sexual commodity, with both humanizing and dehumanizing effects. We moved on to another place, called Bed Supperclub. The waitresses were dressed as nurses and the waiters as doctors, with stethoscopes hanging around their necks. Clients lay on couches or castored beds while the nurses took orders from lovely European youth of both sexes. I was beginning to feel unhinged. Available beauty does not lose its awe, and the Western ego melts very easily, like dirty snow.

Somewhere around five a.m. I found myself driving around the city in a cab, not quite knowing where I was going. One can wander around a city this large without a plan, even in a cab, since a three-hour cab ride rarely costs more than about $10. The city is famously a "jungle" of the as-

phalt variety, but we too infrequently take up the invitation
to treat it like one. The forests of towers, the intertwining
paths like trails, the human fauna—out of the night, glittering *kathoey* in face paint stepped off the curbs toward the
car, signaling their offers—they looked like the spectacularly
decorated Papuan tribesmen so lovingly photographed by
Irving Penn in his book *Passage*. In Thailand, boys have the
legal right to wear skirts at school and the derogatory "fag-
got" is rarely heard on the street. Male dandyism is unex-
ceptional; indeed, it is widely admired. A Buddhist can be
reincarnated as either sex, and there is in the air a taste of
fluidity, of sliding joys, that reaches back obscurely into a
metaphysics that a Westerner can only glimpse.

It is this intangible quality that pervades the metropolis
and makes it into a Wherever that is, paradoxically, a place
unlike any other. Nowhere else would this mad jumble of architectural pastiche styles be enjoyable. In Vegas, for example, it makes you want to weep. But Thais love the style they
call *satai Roman*, what we would call Neoclassical (the Cae-
sar's Palace variety, not the Palladian). The city is sprinkled
with gilded putti somersaulting in canary-yellow fountains,
Greek pediments encrusted with iridescent ceramics, neon-
lit architraves, ceremonial scallops, and fluted Corinthian
columns with the foliage modified to a lotus. Cornwel-Smith
suggests that this love of classical reference is a way of tap-
ping into the prestige that Greece and Rome enjoy even in
the Far East as symbols of order, civility, wealth, philosophy,
discipline, culture, and ethics: "the entire classical idyll,
though perhaps not democracy." He adds, "Upwardly mobile nations go classical to give them an impression of
matching the big powers, which also used it as a stamp of

ownership in their colonies." It was, in fact, the first international style of whereverdom, as Calcutta had shown. As the Oriental showed, too—for old Bangkok has many long, low storefronts decked out in the Sino-Portuguese classical style that was established by Portuguese traders in Malacca centuries ago and that worked its way across Asia over time.

The most florid exemplar in contemporary Bangkok is the Sena Hotel, a riot of Greek caryatids, busily embellished pediments, and soaring Neoclassic windows worthy of the Louvre. We passed it, its arches lit up in gold, and it occurred to me that the city has a genius for mishmosh syncretism. Did that make it beautifully adaptable to the inherent vulgarity of tourism?

Before long, I was making daily trips to Bumungrad Hospital to get my malaria, hepatitis, and dengue fever shots. To be nearer the hospital, I moved to the Conrad Hilton on Wireless Road and made the commute on foot. I would go there even when I didn't have to.

I couldn't help becoming intrigued by the recently changed SRSs wandering around Bumungrad Hospital. They were "tourists" too, in essence. They could even be called the quintessential tourists of our age. They set off looking for a transformation—and boy did they find it. Every afternoon I sat in the Bumrungrad cafés, playing the game of spot-the-sex-change. The SRS unit attached to Bumrungrad is called the Preecha Aesthetic Institute, named for Asia's most famous plastic surgeon, Dr. Preecha Tiewtranon. Dr. Preecha, as he is popularly known, is also perhaps the world's most famous SRS surgeon, a legend among transsex-

uals in the West. Preecha's teams turn out a veritable pro-
duction line of SRS patients. A fair number of these walking
metamorphoses were to be found amid the recovering trans-
plant patients and liposuction beneficiaries, and they were
happy to tell me about their experiences with Dr. Preecha.
None had a bad word to say about him. He was "the god"
of SRS surgery, a "savior," a sort of enlightened, kindly surgical Buddha. But he was also a prince of the beauty trade.
Dr. Preecha, they said, had *the eye*. Although I had resolved
not to go through the predictable routines of a journalistic
interview with anyone, I decided to make an exception for
Dr. Preecha. In a strange way, I was sure he would provide a
critical insight into the inner workings of the Bangkok
tourist machine.

The Web site of the Preecha Aesthetic Institute (PAI) offers a
variety of package holidays to Westerners who wish to
change their sex discreetly for an all-inclusive price. Package
1 shows a girl in a bright yellow bikini leaning against a
New England beach fence and offers free round-trip airport
pickups, five nights in one of the institute's private rooms, all
surgeries and supplies, pre- and postop care, and doctors'
fees. Price: $9,260. This includes Penile Skin Inversion or
Vaginoplasty, Breast Augmentation or Augmentation Mam-
moplasty, and Adam's Apple Contouring. In Package 2, you
pay $12,200 for all this plus a Full Face-Lift. If you dispense
with the face-lift and the Adam's Apple Contouring in Package 3, the price drops to $8,700. And so on.

The PAI is airy and white, with ceramic bowls in niches
and signs that read CHECK UP, GOLDEN AGE, PRE-
MENOPAUSE, 2,950 BAHT. A Chinese girl with a kind of face

splint walked around as if in shell shock. In the Counselor Room, a flat white table held a picture of a bowl of cherries and a cartoon of Dr. Preecha performing tai chi (or was it disco dancing?). Other pictures of dilators completed the minimalist decor, along with a wall of Chinese monkey paintings. A glowing article about the doctor was proudly displayed—from *Pink Ink*, presumably a gay paper.

In came Dr. Preecha, wearing a pair of black slippers. He must have been about sixty, bubbling with merry self-importance. Another cartoon showed him as the "Godfather of Cosmetic Surgery."

"That's me," he said, shaking his head as if disbelieving something.

Bangkok, Preecha maintained, was the best place in the world for cosmetic surgery. Brazil was still good, he admitted, but more expensive than Thailand. In Thailand, it was actually promoted by the government. They wanted the country to be the tourist surgery capital of the world. And medical tourism was booming: look at South Africa, which was pioneering so-called Sun and Surgery packages. Companies there offered a weeklong safari in which a surgical operation was embedded, as it were, painlessly. But Thailand was still cheaper and had just as much sun. "And other things, too." He winked. The problem these days was rising expectations. People wanted to be perfect, especially when it came to sex reassignment. Dr. Preecha's face darkened.

"They say they want eight-inch dick. No, no, I say, not possible. Yes, dicks! Not possible you have eight inch. Moreover"—he guffawed and made a motion like smoking, though there was no cigarette—"if you have poor circulation, flap inside vagina will be *problematic*."

Looking up, I now saw a hitherto unnoticed painting

showing a Thai general whispering into the ear of an old lady. Dr. Preecha's cell phone then rang: a newly arrived *farang* patient calling from the airport.

"Yes, yes. It's hot, isn't it? Just get a taxi . . . no, they won't rob you. No, no. They won't *rob* you. That's right. All right. See you."

He turned to me with a shrug. "A sex-change patient. Man to woman. He's a little nervous."

Who wouldn't be?

"And yet," he said, "it's a relatively simple operation. The appearance is not the problem. It's the insides that are tricky. Almost all the Europeans and Americans are male to female. The Japanese and Chinese are female to male. There are more complications, so we like them to be in the region, you see."

"So all your patients from the West are men?"

"Exactly. And out of three thousand sex-change patients, only one ever changed his mind. Before, I mean."

He laughed like a general, like the general in the picture.

"We're doing forty-five a week now. Mostly from Iran. Yes, the Muslim countries are big customers. The Iranians fill condoms with cash and stick them up their ass. That's how they smuggle the money out to pay for it. Actually, if they go back as a 'miss' it's okay with the Iranian authorities. But our biggest potential market is China. There are five hundred thousand people in China who want to change their sex. Amazing, no? We already have a thousand lined up. We're actually opening a clinic in Shanghai soon."

The optimistic doctor calculates that worldwide one in every sixteen thousand men wants to be a woman. The math is inexorable: Thailand could be making a lot of money in the years to come.

"They are not gays," he went on, raising his voice a little. "One out of thirty thousand women wants to be a man, too. So it adds up to a potentially huge global industry. Three percent of six billion!"

He then looked me over, wondering probably what I was doing here and what he could do for me.

"Not here for a breast implant? That's our most popular business. Breasts. And face-lifts."

"Well, I was thinking about my skin—"

He put on his glasses and peered at my pores for a few moments.

"Yes. But not a face-lift. Not yet." He laughed hoarsely. "Even though we do a good price: thirty-five hundred dollars. It's fifteen thousand in the States. We do the breasts for twenty-five hundred. Ten thousand dollars where you come from."

I shrugged impotently.

"America is *so* expensive." He sighed. "It's ridiculous. Wholly unnecessary. The European health system is so much better than the American. They treat people as patients, not as numbers. The American billing system is so corrupt. People have thirty things on their bill they can't even read."

But wasn't that driving Americans into his arms?

"I am not complaining. And obesity is a huge growth sector. The fatter Americans are, the better for us. Liposuction is exploding." He rapped the table with a kind of military glee. "Exploding!"

Was it true, I asked, that Thais were unusually tolerant of human foibles, of sexual eccentricities in particular, and therefore of aesthetic obsessions?

"Oh, yes. Buddhists make good cosmetic surgeons. We're compassionate pragmatists."

One of the strangest aspects of Preecha's art is the way it

is changing the human face. Asians typically want Caucasian eyes and noses, so after Preecha has provided these for them, they possess faces unlike any seen hitherto. A new kind of human face. And a new kind of body, too. Male fat, he said, is fibrous and difficult to suck out, but female hormones make female fat soft and easily extractable. A new kind of female body was therefore emerging in the twenty-first century—a body with novel contours and textures.

But perhaps I had come to the wrong place, he suggested. For as I now confessed, it was more my internal health that was preoccupying me; my mental health, too—and I explained the trip upon which I was embarked. Papua meant nothing to him, however, until I explained that it was part of Indonesia.

"Ah, primitive." He sighed. But I would probably lose a lot of weight. A jungle trip would be like an extreme spa.

"I would rather lose the weight first," I said.

Dr. Preecha rose, and I rose with him. We began to walk briskly through the dazzling white clinic.

"Have you considered going to a place like Chiva-Som? It's expensive, but it's still a quarter of what you'd pay in the West. It's a scientific nutrition spa in Hua Hin, just down the coast. I would imagine it would be excellent preparation for your ordeal. It will get you used to a fat-free diet, rigorous exercise, healthy thoughts—"

"Healthy thoughts?"

I must have pulled a face, for he shrugged in agreement.

I'd never heard of Chiva-Som, no doubt because I had never considered going to a spa. But now, I reflected, I had a bona fide reason. I wanted to get fitter, leaner, stronger. More jungle-ready.

"It's in Hua Hin, on the coast three hours from Bangkok. I believe your Liz Hurley goes there."

Many cosmetic patients went there, in fact, to recover from their wounds—physical, psychological, or both.

We had now come upon a Japanese girl with fluffy cotton buds stuck to her eyelids. She peered at us like a wounded seal with paralyzed eyelids.

"How are your eyes, Miss Chieko?"

"Me pain."

Dr. Preecha turned to me proudly.

"Another Asian eye patient. They all want eyes like yours." He laughed, I thought, rather pointedly. My own was still puffy and the good doctor had shot it a quick glance. "Miss Chieko, we can take those plasters off tomorrow."

She bowed and tried to smile. Tomorrow she would wake up with Caucasian eyes.

Once resolved to try Chiva-Som, I had to conserve money by leaving the pampered milieu of the luxury hotel. Bangkok abounds in "four-star" places that cost $30 a night instead of $200, and so the economy was nothing if not eminently feasible. But the cramped family hotels along Sukhumvit were not my scene, for there always seem to be pointless arguments at reception between harassed daughters of the owners and irate cheapskate tourists from Portugal or Israel haggling over their local phone charges. There is much shaking of pieces of paper, broken English attempting a suave put-down, and superb stares of contempt from the gorgeous Thai girls, who make it known that *they know* what a barbarian looks like. I prefer the large, anonymous fake-luxury piles constructed around the world in the 1970s when the Soviet Union was still admired. One such place is the Grace on Soi 3, a place that has the added advantage of being a notorious knocking shop for Bangkok's indigent Middle Eastern gentlemen, who shack up there for weeks on end as they try to assuage the desires that their own cultures so spectacularly fail to sate. When you mention the Grace, Thais politely snicker and roll their eyes, a gesture that—miraculously—implies no disapproval whatsoever. The Grace's advantages are also that, with hundreds of cheap rooms, there is no need to book ahead or even phone. All comers are accommodated with perfect anonymous indifference.

The Grace's driveway rises in a curve to a busy series of glass doors thronged with Middle Eastern men talking on cell phones. Inside, the Grace is not just a hotel: it is an erotic installation. In a twenty-four-hour coffee shop, the Arab men sit with their teas and cakes watching plump Thai girls trawling through a lobby fitted with long leather sofas. At the end of this same lobby, an *oud* orchestra plays from eleven p.m. to five a.m. to an Arabian Nights club.

With my new teeth, intestines, skin, and psyche, I was robust enough to endure three nights here to make a grand saving of some $300 or so—enough at least for a night at Chiva-Som at the discounted press rate. There are no frills at the Grace, and none are expected. Surly mama sans patrol the landings, where an incredible number of girls come and go—laughter in the night—and the men seem docile, satisfied, and meekly bashful as they cram together in the tiny elevators. Downstairs, the Arabian Nights was in full swing all night. The walls were lined with yellowed murals of Bernini's Rome. I ordered a cocktail called Knockout. It tasted of anise and, in due course, it knocked me out. As I sipped at it, the orchestra played its Egyptian classics and a beautiful Arab girl pranced around the stage in a blond wig. The Arab men isolated in this high-tech Buddhist city clapped along. Two old men in velvet hats tried clumsily to pick up a pair of young Thais, with much head cocking and bashful smiles, and by the pool tables outside the trade came and went at lightning speed. A stairwell descended from the lobby to a twenty-four-hour Turkish bath from which wisps of steam rose like the fumes of a soft but indisputably pornographic inferno.

THE SPA

Hua Hin lies three hours southwest of Bangkok on the Gulf of Thailand. In the 1920s it was a popular bathing spot for the Thai aristocracy, and the royal family built a summer home here, bringing much of the Bangkok *hoi oligoi* with them. Rama VII still passes much of his time here, sleeping it is rumored by day and working by night. Today, it's a tourist mecca far less known than Phuket or Ko Samui but dominated by the same factors: an international leisure class, a rich spa health sector, towering Hiltons, and girlie bars. Wealthy Thais dominate the last two; foreigners flock to the spas. The beach is flat and ethereal; inland, innumerable square windmills spin over miles of paddies. Patronized by the royals, the town affects an indifference to formality that reveals, paradoxically, a deep love of formality. There are few *farangs* buying sea snails in the night market, but the Thai families in shorts eating squid on the wooden piers have chauffeured Mercedeses waiting for them. Along the beaches, immense American and European resorts sport flaming braziers, tai chi pavilions, and outdoor yoga platforms set among frangipani trees.

Chiva-Som began as a private medical retreat and beach home for the former deputy prime minister, Booncha Rojanestien. Inspired by Champney's spa in Hertfordshire, to which he was a frequent visitor, Rojanestien tore down his summer home and erected this serene replica of a Buddhist monastery. In 1996, it was opened to the public, which is to say to rich Thais. Western celebrities soon followed. Chiva-Som offers a kind of holistic purification based on water treatments and a restaurant serving food designed by a nutritionist: no salt, no sugar, and no oil. In other words, you go there to lose weight.

As befits Thailand's preeminent spa, Chiva is gated, with heavy security. Hua Hin itself is assiduously screened out. Each guest has a detached Thai-style chalet with pointed gables. In the lobby, a small Buddha presides over a rectangular pool dotted with lotus blooms. The word "spa" is an acronym derived from the Latin *salus per aqua*, "health through water," which Roman legionaries believed could cure wounds. (A fourteenth-century town in Belgium later took the name Spa to advertise its water cures.) Chiva-Som decided to go back to the spa's roots in water.

At the resort's heart lies a thalassotherapy center, made of pools, pebbled tunnels, and splashing fountains. Underwater shiatsu is a popular treatment; they call it Watsu. One could call it Ayurvedic Lite with a dash of Switzerland.

The "spa and resort concept," as it's known, has been adopted by most of the hotel brands, from Sofitel and Hilton to Anantara and Marriott, and it acknowledges that tourists are driven as much by the pursuit of personal beauty as by curiosity about other cultures. Virtually every luxury hotel now contains a branded spa on the premises. Indeed, the spa is now a cornerstone of global travel, with a galaxy of brands that merge effortlessly with other brands, whether hotels, cruise lines, or resorts.

The largest supplier of spas worldwide is Steiner Leisure, a British company that started out as a Victorian pharmacy, became a hairdressing salon, and then made its name in the 1960s designing the first seaborne spas for Cunard Line cruise ships. Steiner owns two spa lines, Mandara and El-emis: the first is an Asian spa line that can now be found inside Marriott hotels and on Carnival cruise ships; the latter is a range of beauty products that Steiner manufactures for its own outlets. At the same time, Steiner also operates three beautician campuses in the United States, including the Florida College of Natural Health and the Virginia Massage School, which train technicians to fill "beauty positions" in Steiner companies. Thus, the spa business has its own synergies: campuses, factories, skin care lines, hair products, and spa facilities are all part of a single manufacturing system. The spa itself is not a spiritual retreat, as it pretends to be; it's a self-contained corporate brand coolly aimed at maximizing its profits from what could be called the anxiety of health and beauty. The soothing wave sounds that flow from the company's Web site and the Eastern lore (Mandara Gili, it says, was a sacred mountain that promised eternal life) are wrapping that easily separates form from substance. Steiner posted profits of $341 million in 2004 from 50-odd land spas and 118 cruise ships. Its share performance on NASDAQ is stellar.

In her article "What Fast Food Taught Me about Spa Management," American spa expert and consultant Melinda M. Minton compares the modern spa to food franchises like McDonald's or Bennigan's, made cost-efficient by relentless employee brainwashing and marketing rhetorics. For the luxury medical spa, for example, the problem is how to verbally repackage a humble facial. "If you are a clinical spa,"

Minton suggests, "why not go for a living cell therapy hy-
dration under the multi layer masquing?" Industry seers
now say that the future lies with "medical spas," which are
increasingly being designed with input from resident doctors. And as spas and medicine fuse, spa marketers will
make their language more and more "medical" and biological. Having a massage and a facial will be made to sound
like having some kind of complex (but enjoyable) beauty
surgery. Then there is the sensual displacement of the spa, its
odd similarity to a voyage of some kind. "Offer a temporarily thatched floor. Allow your client to be in Thailand for
ninety minutes. Charge them handsomely for their excursion."

The principle behind "massclusivity," whether in spas or
in resorts in general, is to make the client feel like pampered
royalty alone with his or her pleasures while being processed
through a mildly hedonistic conveyor belt at top speed. It
goes without saying that time can be made to seem much
slower moving in order to amplify the feeling of recupera-
tion. A week can be made to feel like a month, a day like a
week. After all, the economic parsing of time that we have
internalized since childhood falls away abruptly as soon as
we are idle and abroad. For most people, the cessation of
work alone achieves this illusion. In the destination spa, especially, you have *too much* time. Your days are empty, filled
with curious frivolities that you have persuaded yourself are
critical to your health. You float from hour to hour, half
bored, half mesmerized, feeling as if the thousands of dollars
or euros you are spending are a bargain, while they are, of
course, nothing of the sort.

———

The first hours and days at Chiva-Som were almost an out-of-body experience. After the pell-mell of Bangkok, the gated hush of the resort was difficult to acclimatize to. Creamy frangipanis stood around the tilted lawns; small go-carts glided along the paths, ushering visitors from the main gate to their allotted chalets. It was physically arranged as a utopian minivillage or monastery, crossed by these toy-town paths upon which guests did not appear to walk on foot, with the beach behind laid out like a giant mat. Expansive American brand resorts flanked it, though discreetly set back from the beach, their glades sprinkled with fairy lights. The mood was subdued throughout. There were almost no Thai guests that I could see; perhaps noiseless introspection, bed at eleven, and an unsalted fat-free diet was not exactly their idea of a vacation. It is, for that matter, a very Western idea of "health"—the cessation of life.

The second night, lying in my air-conditioned chalet filled with esoteric beauty products, I dreamed that I was sleeping in this same room, but now filled with dozens of empty beds. Slowly, these beds began to fill with fat, sweaty middle-aged couples while my own bed started to shrink, diminishing in size until it became little more than a tiny square upon which I was perched like a stranded seal. I was outraged. I called the management on the phone (the receiver smelled of sandalwood incense) and threatened to leave. "This is supposed to be a relaxing experience!" I screamed at them. "It is relaxing!" they screamed back. "It is not relaxing!" I screamed again. I looked around at the groaning beds: proletarian Czechs. Then, without warning, I woke and found myself alone after all. A shrill human noise filtered through the shutters above the hum of the air conditioner. It was a chorus of female voices chanting, "Kill! Kill!" Peering out over my verandah, I saw a group of Western clients in the yoga pavilion next door thrusting high kicks into the faces of imaginary targets. The morning Thai boxing class. "Kill!" they screamed, and lashed out with their feet.

At eight I had a consultation with Jeff, the Australian nutritionist who analyzes each guest at the beginning of his or her stay. He sat on a rubber Pilates ball behind his desk, bobbing faintly as he looked over my charts.

"We aim for six hundred and sixty calories per meal, totally fat free. We can offer some Ayurvedic treatments alongside if you like—have you ever tried *neti*, the sinus-cleaning workout? It's with a watering can."

"Never."

He bounced a little on his rubber ball and cocked his head. "It's amazing. So is *chi nei tsang*, Chinese stomach massage. Our regime here is totally based on the digestive system. Stress in your gut is usually the root of your problems. Now, colonic irrigation—"

I raised a hand to stop him.

"Yes," he argued, "but it has to be weeklong. You have to remember that we suffer from what I call the disorders of affluence. It's too much good living that is breaking us down from the inside. We eat out all the time—business lunches, expense accounts—"

He tutted and the ball wobbled. He made the business lunch sound like a comet hitting the earth.

"I've never been to a business lunch," I protested.

An acupuncturist stopped in for a moment. They discussed a case—a celebrity, it would seem, from the lowered voices. Then he resumed: "In the West, we're sedentary by the time we're forty. It's a disaster. So we try to reverse this disaster by reversing your eating mistakes. As I said, six hundred and sixty calories—"

He explained that their only rival in the world of elite spas was Canyon Ranch in the United States. But unlike that fabulous facility, Chiva-Som was truly global. There were more Russians here than Thais. And what I had to remember was that my week there was not the usual vacation. He made quotation marks in the air with his fingers. No, Chiva-Som didn't offer "vacations." It offered transformations.

"Club Med doesn't change anyone, does it?"

I shook my head sadly. No it didn't.

"No other tourist experience can change people like this one. Chiva will change you for six months after you leave. Some people are transformed for life." His expression became quite evangelical at the thought of these converted souls. "We wean people off their past lives. It's a synergy of exercise, nutrition, relaxation, and therapy. And no French food." He didn't laugh. "French food kills you."

Does it? I thought.

"No French food, and lots of water therapy."

I was then weighed and my body fat ratio assessed. I confessed that after three operations in Bangkok, my teeth were aching a bit.

"Stress." He sighed. "You'll feel much better in a few days."

He drew up a program for me, and I felt suddenly relieved to have a Plan. For once, my eating and exercising would not be random or arbitrary, but organized and profound. They would proceed according to scientific principles. They would be a transformational conversion to a higher level of beauty, which is tantamount in our culture to a higher level of sainthood.

I was surely stressed, as Jeff had intimated. But I was stressed mostly by the fact that I now had nothing to do all day and that I nevertheless had to find things to do. I put on my bathrobe and silk slippers and padded down the pathway to the thalassotherapy spa. Usually there was no one there, not even a damsely neurotic to flirt with, and I could flounder around the series of hot and cold pools and explore curved passageways floored with sea pebbles where the water came to the knee. It was very *satai Roman*, harking back to the classical baths without the kitsch of a Bangkok sauna. Statues of Apollo or the Discobolus would have gone down well here, but then so would the attendants of a Bangkok sauna. Alas, there was neither. In the sauna, I lay on the stone benches and wondered how it was that a spa could be so lonely. The Roman bath, after all, was a place of male conviviality, of extended conversations. Here, it was a setting for brooding, isolated souls pondering their navels and attempting to revive their flagging life force. But then again, the solitude of this dripping den might be preparing me for more severe adventures.

I redressed in my very Roman robe and sauntered through the pillared lobby to the main pool, whose surface was strewn with peach-colored blossoms. Four or five Western women lay tanning on the beds, attended by uniformed youths with towels and bottled water. There was a heavy air of dejection, of pointlessness, but to swim through flowers is never entirely pointless.

I then went to the beach, which lay beyond a low parapet
at the bottom of a flight of steps. A company cop stands by
the concrete steps, saluting each guest, a tap to one of those
peaked military junta hats that Thai parking lot attendants
and hotel guards love to wear. It was like a Saharan beach,
like the vast strand at Cap Sim in Morocco where the sand
never seems to end in either direction. Single spa women
walked up and down with the same bathrobes as myself,
splashing in the low waves. Each one seemed lost in melancholy, isolated and withdrawn among the chattering Thai
families. Thais do not go to a high-end spa to lose weight or
fast; they go to pamper themselves with French food and
$500 mud baths. We, on the other hand, go to Thai spas to
find a monkish austerity. The women all carried depressingly
thick books. I saw one carrying *Buddenbrooks*. They stared
with a faint disdain at the idle rich spilling out from the
Hyatt next door but also, I would have to admit, at me. I
thought of striking up a conversation—for was there not a
comradeship of the common Chiva-Som bathrobe?—but the
vibe was distinctly icy. The Thai girls trawling the beach, on
the other hand—

Where there is nothing to do, one spends a great part
of the day thinking about lunch. Lunch looms large as a
tremendous event, a festivity in the midst of nothingness, a
hiatus in the droning flow of hours. When lunchtime came,
I therefore felt an exaggerated relief. Situated in an elegant
first-floor colonial-style salon, the restaurant served biomet-
ric meals from several circular buffets. Around these arrays
of sprouts and greens, of exotic plant life and rare fruits, the
guests assemble with an awkward complicity that never
breaks down into mutual amiability. The tables are set indi-

vidually and "privacy" is scrupulously respected—enforced, even. The women from the beach reappeared with their thick books, their skin glistening unhealthily. (Were *they* invalids?) They ate plates of spartan proportions, little piles of alfalfa with a few chopped nuts, and tall glasses of sugarless lemonade. They concentrated as they chewed, a picture of tense apprehension. A fat Indian businessman and his equally fat wife moved with slow, crablike circumspection around this calorie-controlled food and their expressions were equally tense. "Rabbit food," I heard him mutter. Heavy sunglasses disguised potential celebrities. Bit by bit, the wonderful glamour of the word "lunch," the glorious history of lunch, seeped away and I was left with this dry smorgasbord of sprouts and cress that was doing wonders for my liver, an organ I never see and that therefore plays only a subordinate role in my psyche.

At two, I abandoned lunch and went to the Watsu pool for an appointment with my "water therapist." The ritual is fixed and meticulously timed, like most of what happens at Chiva-Som. To the sound of soothing New Age tunes, you get into a deep, hot pool, where a muscular Thai looking a little like Yukio Mishima awaits you. He *wai*'s and tells you "not to worry." Closing your eyes and floating on your back, you are twirled around in a marine ballet; you are twisted into therapeutic underwater shapes, sloshed around by your feet, caressed, and numbed. An hour passes and gradually you lose all sense of reality. You have no idea where you are or who this mystic masseur is. You are totally disoriented, and therein lies your luxury. You wonder if you are drowning or sailing through air. You wonder whether

you should be aroused, or whether you are. The therapist
smiles and says things like, "You let go human body."

That night I sat in the outdoor restaurant next to the
beach, watching pink *khong fai* lanterns floating high in the
sky, candles shimmering like static comets. The reader of
Buddenbrooks sat at the next table. Willowy, tortured, with
a Nikita haircut—French by the look of it. Two women in
pink sarongs and hideous straw hats sipped chamomile tea
by the pool. Their voices were louder, coarser—English.
Guests come to Chiva to be alone, to find solitude. And yet,
just beyond the nocturnal trees, the joyous clatter of Hua
Hin town could be felt. It was a strange seclusion. It seemed
like the solitude of the Western woman itself—a room of
one's own, far from the madding diet and even more madding husbands.

A rake-thin figure came loping across the pool area in a
black suit and tie. Surprisingly, Paul Linder, Chiva's Swiss director, was not sweating at all. But I had to ask him why he
was wearing a suit.

"It's a question of respect," he replied. "The employees
see me in a suit and tie, and they know I mean business."

The officials of global tourism are not unlike those
doughty standard-bearers of vanished European empires
who sweated through the tropic days in stiff stand-fall collars and tiepins, more conscious of their status as icons than
of their chugging sweat glands. And like those heroic bu-
reaucrats, they are a class of uprooted global citizens who
have progressively lost their sense of national belonging.
Tourism after all is the ultimate global enterprise, and it demands from its workers a globalized consciousness. And as
with imperialism, many of its functionaries and administra-
tors cast a cold eye on its excesses. Linder worked in Korea,

at the Normandie restaurant at the Bangkok Oriental, in Sydney, and in San Moritz. He never thought he would be running a spa. Or making a living from transnational tourism.

"Tourism can be a terrible thing," he admitted, as we watched the lanterns disappear into the stratosphere. "The locals here are destroying themselves with greed. The Hyatt next door is sad." He looked over scornfully at the glow of a thousand tree lanterns where the Hyatt entertained its masses. "But it's fifty percent of the Thai economy. Fifty percent is a lot."

Hua Hin used to depend on the shrimp business. But why man a shrimp boat when you can tend frangipani trees at the Hyatt for more? Or work in a spa? Linder frowned.

"We don't particularly like the word 'spa.' Chiva isn't really a spa. We prefer to call it a Health and Wellness Resort."

Again, he repeated the idea that such a resort offered a transformational experience.

"An *experience*," he insisted. "Not just fun."

But is experience superior to fun? Fun, in any case, is also an experience.

Every night, after sitting alone on the restaurant terrace looking forlornly at the ethereal women, I went to bed at nine and slept as deeply as only a displaced urban insomniac can. My dreams now ran clear; I woke at first light and joined the kick-boxing class. All morning I sat in the Water Therapy Suites or pondered my intestinal health in the restaurant. I rode the golf carts back and forth and took a sugarless lemonade at the pool. For whole hours I lost any sense of being in Thailand at all, or even in the Far East. That was the idea. The advantage of its being in Thailand, for many guests, was simply the cost: $500 a night instead of $1,300.

But as the days passed, I began to feel a nagging itch. At night, I wandered down the beach to the Hyatt. Yes, it was the unacceptable face of high-end mass tourism, and the food they served under their groves of illuminated trees was not designed to enhance one's natural peristalsis. But it smelled good. I began to prowl through their opulent grounds, drawn by the scents of fat-fried Thai food unencumbered by a single stalk of alfalfa. Here were plump couples in tourist uniforms slouched in poolside deck chairs with plates of sautéed prawns. Here was a water bar where a smiling man made huge margaritas with liquefied kiwis. Would it be a betrayal of Chiva-Som, I wondered, if I sat here for a half hour and drank a kiwi margarita? Would I be seen and reported to Dr. Jeff?

One night as I was doing my Watsu, I felt the first pricking of a forbidden craving. It was a simple lust, and one to which I am serially prone. I see in my mind's eye a heavy china plate upon which has been arranged a steak seared only on the outside, accompanied by a simple garnish of crisply turned fries, long, thin, slightly charred, and very heavily salted. The salt of the fries will serve as that of the steak, for a top steak needs nothing by way of condiment. Next to this Dutch Realist apparition worthy of Vermeer stands a bottle of Volnay from a producer like Michel Lafarge, which is to say made with nary a bow to cretinous "market laws" or gumdrop anglophone tastes. You will not find this tableau at the Hua Hin Hyatt Regency, but that is the general idea. I could certainly get a steak with a bottle of Penfolds.

But after a few explorations of the Hyatt, my fantasy returned. The wine list was shit and the steak I observed while passing a table didn't look exactly sensational. The place was soporific—Hawaii on the Gulf of Thailand. If I was going to transgress, it would be better to go the whole hog and escape into Hua Hin itself. Leaving the saintly premises of Chiva-Som on foot, therefore, I wandered down to the guardhouse on the road and asked the two guards how I could get to Hua Hin. They looked taken aback in the extreme and tried to dissuade me from even trying. No one from Chiva-Som, they pointed out, went to Hua Hin late at night. Hua Hin was for locals, for Thais. But if I insisted, they grudgingly supposed that I could catch a passing tuk-tuk into town. It was strongly not recommended. And they drew themselves up as if about to utter an even sterner warning. Were they actually going to prevent me going to Hua Hin?

"I absolutely must go to Hua Hin," I cried. I might have added: "I am dying of virtue!"

The tuk-tuk driver nodded in sympathy.

"You wa' good meat now?"

"Yes! Steak—shrimp—anything!"

"Purple Pussy Club?"

"No, no: shrimp. *Scwhimp*."

He dropped me at the Hua Hin town piers, rickety wooden spits piled high with food stalls. In seconds, the human heat of Thailand was back in my lungs, and with waves churning below me I gorged on a greasy bowl of shrimp noodles.

The place was pandemonium; a hundred hookers from the street eating *guaydio naam* with plastic chopsticks. I began downing Singha beers. Then grilled prawn satay, *hormor* with snakehead fish, and *plad curry extreme hot*. Sweat poured down my face, dropping into the bowl, and I guzzled various liquids infused with the fats of dead beasts, landbound and otherwise.

I thought of Dr. Jeff bouncing on his Pilates ball. What is a world without fat? To compare the fat of pudgy prawns to that of sizzling chicken bits, to sink into flavored fats tossed around in fatty woks, to suck up fats shot through with blinding-hot chilies, fats consisting of green blobs and oil slicks of reddish brown. Fats creamy as mashed tofu, fats floating on top of broths.

I realized then that I was in a dire state of fat withdrawal. With the sudden intake of hot fat, however, I felt my whole body relax ecstatically. I took another tuk-tuk around town. The whole place was partying; in the cavernous lobby of the Hilton Hua Hin, bands of girls in tank tops danced to a wretched band. In the street, they came running after the tuk-tuk, waving madly. "You bad man, you come back now!" When I compared them to the pasty, anxious women locked up inside Chiva-Som, I felt only a twinge of sadness. Life is elsewhere.

Such is the thoroughness of the spa system, however, that I could not escape a final reckoning at the hands of Dr. Jeff, a kindly soul all in all. On one's last day, there is a weighing, an overview assessment, a progress report, and some final recommendations that one can take back into the real world. It is generally expected that over the course of a one-week treatment the average guest can lose three or four pounds if he or she exercises vigorously every day. And why come to Chiva-Som if you are not prepared to profit from it to the maximum degree? My final reckoning was therefore all the more disappointing insofar as we discovered that I had actually *gained* weight. A few eyebrows were raised and some hard questions were posed concerning the seriousness of my commitment to self-improvement, inner equilibrium, and intestinal rigor. I admitted that intestinal rigor was not really my thing. I could have gone on about the steak and the Volnay, but mentioning French food did not seem like an appropriate move. It would be taken as a death wish. Dr. Jeff looked at me with mercilessly compassionate, as if about to voice some dark suspicion.

Instead, he merely asked, "Where do you go from here?"

I told him I was on my way to Bali.

"Lucky man. It's a fabulous place. Many great spas on Bali."

"I won't be going to any of them."

I was going, I said, for a rendezvous with the man who would be taking me into the heart of New Guinea.

"Is that a very moral thing to do?" he asked quite reasonably. "I mean, visiting a Stone Age people like that? I would have second thoughts."

I did have second thoughts. What would be the truest reply to his question? That the premise of visiting a supposedly uncontacted people seemed, so far, both dubious and unsettling; that I knew Papua was bound *not* to be the Eden that many an ecological tourist must assume it to be.

"It's a tough place. We used to rule Papua New Guinea." He spoke as an Australian, of course, and his voice went cool. "The diet will be good for you, though. Sago palms, isn't it?"

PARADISE MADE

Denpasar has one of the most refined airports in the world, with the mood of a provincial museum blended with a singsong holiday camp. Its halls are richly adorned with displays of Balinese high culture; classical gamelan music is piped—not too loudly—into every available public space, creating a subconscious background atmosphere that quickly evokes girls dancing in gold headdresses and snapping their painted fingers. Mossy temples, you think idiotically, mystical shrines in the mountains, sacred volcanoes, a harmonious spiritual paradise. This eerie music is everywhere—on the elevators, at the immigration booths, in the luggage hall, and throughout the arrivals lounge. It sounds like a serpentine tune that is repeated over and over, a gamelan playing in tandem with a flute. You will find yourself submerged in this same tune everywhere you go in Bali, as if the island had to have a single respectable soundtrack to establish its mood. It is ringing in your ears by the time you have persisted into the parking lot and the heat of the equator bursts upon your skin. It is clear what the subliminal message is: we are an Island of Culture. Culture is what we do. We are Cultural. Refinement is the air we breathe. The word "paradise" is virtually everywhere. From one brochure:

The island of Bali has long been characterized in the West as the last "paradise" on earth; a traditional society insulated from the modern world and its vicissitudes, whose inhabitants are endowed with exceptional artistic talents and consecrate a considerable amount of time and wealth staging sumptuous ceremonies for their own pleasure and that of their gods— now also for the delectation of foreign visitors!

It is even hotter than Bangkok. The Australian families are all around you, the children carrying their blow-up water wings and beach balls, and the Anglo-Saxon look is back in the foreground: tattoos, buzz cuts, cut-off shirts, hideous shorts. They clearly don't give a shit about Bali culture, or any culture, for that matter. They are here for the beaches of Kuta and of Seminyak. And—if they have money—the Golden Triangle, a vast luxury hotel zone to the far south of the island. It is impossible that they can have any solid notion of what Bali is or was. For of all tourist destinations in the world, Bali is the most decontextualized. It has been rendered thus by the Indonesian authorities themselves, for it is Indonesia's Golden Calf, its splendid money machine, the only place in this enormous nation that Westerners ever visit. The rest of Indonesia, after all, is Muslim and often radical, and the far east of it is Papua. Only Bali beckons the hedonist. And for Bali to be attractive, it must be contentless. "Hindu Disneyland," locals will sometimes call it. The terrorist bombs that killed 202 tourists in a Kuta nightclub in 2002 and those in Kuta and Jimbaran in 2005 were an assault on this unusual fabrication—but the Bali brand, as one might call it, is so deep, so old, and so handsomely fashioned that it will take a lot more than a few jihadist bombs to shake it.

I took a cab into Seminyak. It's a languorous resort spread out along a busy beach, the south end of which is Kuta. Where Kuta is raucous, vulgar, and intensely youthful, Seminyak is a little quieter, its hotels made in traditional styles and often set back from the beach in perplexing complexes that look from the outside like temples. I had the fanciful notion of checking into one of these for a few days and, slowly acclimatizing to the heat, practicing with my fifty-pound jungle load on the beach every day. This would doubtless make me the local Robinson Crusoe type, bizarrely clad and wild-eyed, and I would probably be tailed mercilessly by the catamitic hustlers for which Seminyak Beach is so justly renowned. But I did not want anyone else to carry my pack in Papua, and to be able to offer myself this noble gesture, I would have to train. My idea was to get up at dawn every day and haul my pack down to the beach, then trudge down as far as Kuta and back again. Since Bali is only four hours' flying time from Papua and on the same line of longitude, I assumed that this preparation would stand me in good stead. I could train my muscles and pores to accept a grueling regime.

The Anipura Villas is a midlevel hotel catering to working-class German and Dutch tourists, who come in fairly large groups and bestir themselves little. For one thing, it is too hot; for another, the Anipura has a dreamy pool surrounded by frangipanis and with a view over rice paddies that appear through every crevice of Seminyak's sprawling suburbia. Silhouettes of mountains came into view in the morning, before the rains came crashing down. The same flute and gamelan music played around the pool area night and day. A crippled Dutch man, the victim of some terrible industrial accident, was lowered into the water by his wife. The Balinese attendants watched them all impassively; they were too young for the Dutch tones to recall the former colonial master. Swimming there under the moon with no one around was cheaply beautiful, offering the seduction of obviously contrived illusions.

At night, the main street that connects Seminyak and Kuta is a partially lit ribbon of tourist shops, bars, declining clubs, eateries, and Internet cafés. The Islamists have left their mark, however, for part of the crowds had been sliced away, leaving many joints empty and listless, a tout outside standing forlornly with a menu, pointing to a room of empty tables. Australian women still trawl the sidewalks for male hookers, the so-called Kuta Cowboys, and Kuta is still something of a female Bangkok. Just as in Bangkok you see the hopelessly subpar Western man, sometimes in a wheelchair, holding upon his arm a cheerful supermodel, so in Kuta the loveless white woman finds her long-haired gigolo: the polite compassion of Asia. The long streets of T-shirt shops packed with swimwear look like a red-light zone until you get up close. There are healthy blond couples everywhere; the hustlers brush your arm lightly, with feminine hands, whispering something about dope and young girls.

Before long, I was rising at the exact moment that the moon began to disappear and walking the beach with my pack. It was a long hike. Northward, it took me across shallow rivers cut into the sand, past perennial forest and private

homes, discreet little luxury hotels and alleys bushy with
flowers. To the south, the scene was more industrially
touristy. Even at dawn there were hustlers strolling the
sands, looking for men to pick up. In Bali, it seems, only the
men sell themselves publicly for sex. At the Kuta end, there
are volleyball nets, old masseuses in conical hats, gaggles of
mopeds, and the infrastructure of what looks like a California beach city, culminating in a huge Hard Rock Café complex. Facing it there is a chilling revolutionary statue of the
independence war hero "Jagarana" holding a pistol in one
hand and a flag in the other, signed by one Professor Doctor
Ida Bagus Oka—reminder that even Bali has a political history buried deep under its Western surfaces. By the time I
got to Kuta that first morning I was shattered and took a
motorbike back to the hotel. Eventually, I managed the return hike, followed all the way by the "cowboys" whistling
and telling me how nice their cocks were.

There comes a time, about twenty-four hours after your
arrival, when Kuta fatigue sets in. It's the Paddy's Pub, the
"Auld Lang Syne" played on electric guitars as if to compete
with the piped gamelan music, the puppy-fat blond girls
with beaded hair, the old women with massage licenses
pinned to their hats, the McDonald's offering Idul Fitri
meals; or else the endless K Stores, the half-naked white men
looking like convicts on a spree, with Chinese and barbed-
wire tattoos on their shoulders, and the Bali Barrel surf
shops and the Beer Gardens. It is not the Bali of lore, the
land of villages celebrated by Jane Belo and Gregory Bateson. During the afternoons, I began taking long car rides
along the southern coast, seeking an alternative to the resort
zone. On a small island everything is compressed, even the

countryside. As the suburbs of Kuta peter out, the road winds its way through semiarid scrubland of the Bukit Peninsula, blinding white as Spain, through steeply sloped forests with views of the sea and villages with a single *warung* with red plastic tables. In places it flattens out like a cactus desert.

Bali's tourist economy has been structured as a triangular affair comprising, to the north, the inland city of Ubud, and to the south Kuta and its outlying beaches such as Legian, Sanur, and Seminyak, and the more exclusive peninsula of Nusa Dua. The three "points" of this triangle correspond to three antagonistic types of tourism. Ubud was developed to attract better-educated travelers seeking contact with Bali's classical heritage, while also indulging in exclusive spas; Kuta-Legian would draw in the mass-market beach crowd, and Nusa Dua would appeal to high-end sun worshippers seeking an all-inclusive, heavily fortified vacation in a megaresort along American lines. Bali needs all three, since tourism accounts for some seventy percent of its economy and employs one in five of the population. The Nusa Dua development was begun in 1973 with World Bank funding and was intended to draw off masses that might otherwise overwhelm fragile Ubud. All around this southern region, however, tourism has become the landscape, and vice versa. The villas perched high to capture the sea views and the elite miniresorts that think themselves far from madding crowds are packed into a setting that would be Homeric if they were not there, for here the flat beaches turn into a Mediterranean scene of tortured cliffs and metallic scrub. One road passes the surfer beaches whose repute rings loud in Australia, notably Dreamland but also, to the far south, Ulu Watu.

Inland, the road goes through an extraordinary place, the future Garuda Wisnu Kencana Cultural Park. The GWK, though it sounds like a Soviet factory from its initials, is to be Bali's largest ever tourist development, based according to its builders on "local wisdom." There was nothing to be seen there now, but my driver explained that this giant park resort would one day boast the world's largest sculpture, a 250-foot-tall figure of Vishnu, the Hindu protector god, riding on the bird Garuda. All this will be mounted on a 230-foot-tall pedestal worthy of Albert Speer. It is to be a national monument "sustainable for centuries," just like Speer's projects for Berlin, and like these latter might well never be built. Monumentalism and insecurity jostling together. A few miles on, the same could be said of Nusa Dua: it was like approaching a city-state separated from the rest of Bali by gates, police, and suburbs—in this case, the shambling town of Bualu, where the thousands of service workers for the hotels lived. It was a World Bank project—enough said.

The megaresorts of Nusa are connected like the government buildings of Calcutta by sweeping boulevards framed by lawns and tropical gardens. An army of peasants keeps it all trim. The lobbies of the hotels are outrageous in scale, especially that of the Grand Hyatt and the Sheraton Laguna, though the Nusa Dua Beach Hotel & Spa boasts fragments of re-created Balinese temples. I thought of Lorbrulgrud, the capital of Brobdingnag in *Gulliver's Travels*, that great satire of travel writing. The Hyatt, I calculated at once, must be at least four *glonglungs* long and about as large as the king of Brobdingnag's formidable palace. In fact, I have always wondered whether megaresort architects are also fans of

Gulliver's Travels, for they appear to have borrowed liber-
ally from Swift's inspirations. Floating cities, magical islands, palaces large as English counties, kings and queens
living in absolutist madness. I wandered through the empty
lobby of the Hyatt, grand as a Hearst castle, where a band
played to no one, and then down to the lagoon pool that
stretched all the way to a distant beach. Set amid this
utopian sprawl, the hundreds of units rising on all sides did
indeed seem like a Gulliverian metropolis, but with almost
no one in it. A few Russian girls sat by the pool bar in curious bodysuits, smoking and watching out for their men. At
the heart of this complex sits a thing called the Pasar Seng-
gol, a kind of artisanal Balinese theme park that features a
"night market" and food stalls. Artisans sit around chipping
at sculptures and dabbing at traditional paintings, as if in a
village square, while the stalls do their best to seem ram-
bunctious amid so much sterilized order. The inhabitants of
Nusa almost never venture into the rest of Bali, so the rest of
Bali has to be brought to them, flute and gamelan music included. I settled in here awkwardly and got myself a plate of
vegetable stew called *gado gado* and a beer. Couples drifted
in from the beach, the hard faces of proletarian Northern Europe, cocky Slavs, a few timorous Americans who
thought they were venturing into an enclave of genuine rus-
ticity. On a dismal little beach, attendants were already
straightening out the plastic sunbeds and the parasols.

The following day I drove up to Ubud. It's an hour's drive
across the sprawl of Denpasar and up into the hills. The
road is a remarkable spectacle, not because anything of the

terraced paddies remains on view to either side of it but because it is lined on either side for its entire length by sculpture workshops and display rooms hawking every conceivable facet of Balinese tradition. There are Garudas, freakish Vishnus, mythological creatures, lintels, beds, carved tables, metal lamps, screens, kitchenware, temple altars, timber lion figures, entire ceremonial gates, and garden steles. For a moment, passing through the great traffic circles of Denpasar with their flocks of mopeds, you have a taste of the wider Indonesia, but toward Ubud the tourist rarefication sets in. It rained hard in the uplands, and I could barely see the first courtyard gardens and the drenched flame vines standing at the edge of Ubud's famously photogenic paddy terraces. I took a hotel room off the road to Penestanan, which cuts right through the town, and in the afternoon walked down to the Tutmak Café near the central football field to meet Kelly Woolford, Mr. Papua, as the expat Americans in Ubud sometimes call him.

Ubud is more like an ad hoc settlement consisting of private arrangements than a town in the Western sense. It tumbles up and down ravinelike streets, infested with tourist boutiques and hundreds of hotels. It is filled with temple spaces where Balinese dance is performed almost every night, so repetitively that after a few nights you begin to take it as a three-dimensional backdrop that never goes away. At the Tutmak, however, the expats gather every evening as if escaping the doses of "Bali" that are meted out on every street corner. Woolford showed up in the rain, a waiflike man with one lazy eye and a gentle humor that was turned like a weapon onto his own condition—a forty-one-year-old exile living in a Hindu Disneyland and making a living tak-

ing wealthy clients on harrowing tours in the interior of
Papua. Ubud, he said strenuously, had its advantages. The
women were not American; the food was exquisite and
cheap. There were worse places in which to anchor a wan-
derlust.

We sat by an open window, the rain breathing on our
faces.

"Ubud is like a dollhouse," he admitted. "But, you know,
as a base for Papua, it's *the* place."

Papua is a neighboring province to Bali, but there is not
the slightest trace of it in Bali's tourist spectacles or stores.
Bali is centered uniquely upon itself. In part, this is because
Bali plays a special cultural role in modern Indonesia—it is
seen as a museumlike repository of ancient Javanese culture.
This was the role that the Dutch colonial authorities gave to
it, and it is the role that Indonesia's first president, Sukarno,
also gave to it. His mother, after all, had been Balinese.

Nevertheless, I suddenly felt closer to Papua. Woolford's
vibe was not Balinese or Ubud expat. There was a different
look in his eye, which seemed to pierce right through me. He
chain-smoked as we watched the rain pounding down on a
soggy twilight football match. Despite a degree in criminol-
ogy from Missouri State, he immediately brings to mind an
American backwoodsman of centuries past, complete with
shoulder-length blond hair and the remnants of a Missouri
accent. Something marked him off from everyone else there,
from every other expat type that I could see. The laughter
that was not as loud, the gestures that were not as pronounced somehow, the drifting eye. He had spent a lot of his
life in the Papua forest, pushing his endurance farther and
farther as he found more remote regions that did not show

up even on military maps or GPS topographies. Something made him go back serially over a period of fifteen years. These were brutal, primitive trips, more primitive in some ways than those of Lewis and Clark or the complicated expeditions launched into the interior of Africa in the 1860s. For Woolford journeys were solitary treks often made with a single tracker or guide, often his trusted Papuan friend William. They traveled light—a pot, a tent, a few bits and pieces. The two of them would take a canoe and vanish up a river system without weapons for weeks at a time. The peoples living far upriver on the northern coast of Irian Jaya were sometimes far off ethnography's map and he had met peoples whose name no Papuan of his acquaintance could recognize and whose language was equally unrecognizable. As he related some of these marvelous ventures, I began to notice the childlike relish at the back of his voice, the love of tall stories and magical events. Papua was a place where the instinct for such things—the craving for them—could be indulged. It was "unfathomable, limitless." It could not be tamed or flattened out, not even by the forces of the rest of the world, which itself was hideously flattened—as our prophet of globalization, Thomas Friedman, has suggested in an altogether more Panglossian spirit. If our world was flat, Papua was round. It had flesh and depth. Its savagery could not be reformed. It was the far side of the looking glass, a parallel world about which Indonesians and Westerners could make only strictly fraudulent images.

A few months earlier, he had taken a BBC film crew to a few tree houses he knew in the Korowai-Kombai area for a series called *Going Tribal*. Bruce Parry, the Brit in front of the camera, had gone through all the more grueling Papuan rituals and ordeals, eating sago grubs and bird's eyes, having his nose pierced with a sago thorn, that sort of thing. Hilarious. It made Papua look tamely "awful" for a TV audience, but of course there was nothing in it. The BBC had gone in neurotic, protected, and unadventurous, and the Papuans had played along as good sports. I grudgingly confessed I'd seen the Bruce Parry show and laughed my socks off. Another hapless Limey in the forest.

"But still, I felt bad about the BBC thing. What horseshit."

"Is it because we can't stand to think there is a place we don't dominate? So that even if we don't really dominate it we can humble it by making it into spectacle?"

"That's exactly it, man. Whereas Papua is *something else*. You can't film it. How can you film it?"

There was the Irish writer, Redmond O'Hanlon, who had written about Irian Jaya. And there was the American writer Tobias Schneebaum, who had lived among the Asmat of the south coast in the 1950s and recorded his time there in *Wild Man* and *Where the Spirits Dwell*. Schneebaum, a controversial Eisenhower-era homosexual and a friend of Norman Mailer, had actually ventured inland from the Asmat in the 1970s and encountered a remote Kombai in the deep forest, at a time when the Kombai were virtually unknown—official contact with them wasn't made until 1979. For the documentary *Keep the River on Your Right*, the New York filmmakers Laurie and David Shapiro had taken him back to the Asmat in 1998, where he had rediscovered an old Papuan lover.

"But," Woolford said, "that wouldn't be the Papua I know. The Asmat are fantastic people, the greatest carvers in the South Seas, but it's touristified now. I wouldn't take you there."

In the film we see Schneebaum working on a tourist boat plowing between Bali and Papua, giving lectures about the Asmat to the giggling horde and trying to enjoy the onboard pool. "I dislike tourism," he says at one point, "but it's a living. I have always been broke and I prefer it that way." So he was like Woolford to some degree. Woolford's last client to Papua had been a British investment banker who had thanked him afterward for changing his life. They had gone in alone to the Kombai, and the banker—a man bored with all other touristic venues—had rediscovered his taste for life. The very rich are often like that.

"Because everywhere is like everywhere now. It's all a bore."

"So they want a transformation?"

"Don't we all? Well, the romantics among us. I like that idea of rediscovering a taste for life."

He patiently rolled a cigarette. One could deduce the rest of the thought's vector: "We've fucked the world up comprehensively. It's a shit hole almost everywhere now." In the rain, the Balinese slipped around the goalposts, laughing as they became invisible. The amiable decor of the Tukmak could have been in San Diego, as could most of the clientele. It seemed pretty obvious that an American could live in Ubud with ease, without the friction of strangeness. It was a cheap alternative to the rat race back home. But Woolford's reasons had more to do with Papua. You couldn't live in Papua, that was too radical, too wearying. No Internet connection, for one thing, and so impossible to run a business from there. But it was only four hours from here.

"Which," he said, "is difficult to grasp."

After our drink, I went up alone to the junction of Monkey Forest Road and Jalan Raya, Ubud's main intersection near to which stand the Ubud Palace and temples like the Pura Desa Ubud and the Merajan Agung. Temples on one side of the street, chic bistros on the other. It was now night, and dance performances were starting up in the temple grounds. These traditional dances are the only form of nightlife in Ubud outside of a desultory bar scene. Instead of discos and strip clubs, it's Rangda and Barong dances enacting ancient myths.

It was one of these that I sat down to watch next to the Ubud Palace. Rangda is a witch figure who threatens pestilence on a country; she is shown as a demon with a three-foot tongue, straw hair, and breasts that hang down to her waist. Her rival is the Barong, a priest who takes the magical form of a kind of Chinese lion. The two battle it out while acolytes of the Barong try to attack the Rangda, who uses her magical power to make them turn their daggers—or krisses—against themselves. Like the audience, I was soon lost. If this was the heart of Balinese culture, I and we had no idea what it consisted in. I recalled, though, that Mead had loved these same Rangda and Barong dances when she lived in Ubud and that she had even taken the witch as a central figure in her anthropology of Bali, explored in books like Balinese Character. She had also encouraged Jane Belo to study the mysterious trances that occurred during performances. The dance eventually became the most loved and studied of all Balinese forms. Photographers of the pre-war years, like Thilly Weissenborn, featured them over and over. Gradually, dance became Bali's signature—its traveling dancing troupes were the first thing the West saw of the island in New York and London.

Mead was not the only lover of Rangda dances. They were also much studied by the German artist Walter Spies, who reproduced their sinister ambience in his paintings of Bali life in the 1930s. And it is not by accident that the tourist authorities in Ubud now stage such dances—their centrality, as it turns out, owes everything to Mead and Spies. This is also true of Ubud itself. For if Ubud is today the center of Bali's cultural tourism, it was this charming German homosexual who made it that. As the Bali scholar Adrian Vickers says, "Single-handedly Spies made Ubud the alternative area for genteel tourism, the center of an artistic lifestyle."

It's often assumed that tourism is a system that is imposed by large economic concerns, usually hotel and resort chains, and with a brutal suddenness in the postwar era. Bali shows that this is not always the case. For Ubud, the island's heart, grew out of the enthusiasms of a small circle of artists, writers, musicians, and anthropologists.

It was they who created the "magic" Bali that has now become its dominant image. Clifford Geertz once wrote that Bali was the greatest treasure-house of magical beliefs and customs in Asia. The intellectuals who flocked there in the late 1920s and 1930s would have agreed. They wanted a paradise of archaic belief centered on a village culture, and they largely found what they were looking for. As Geoffrey Robinson, a scholar of Balinese political history, puts it:

It was during these years of the *Pax Neerlandica*, as some colonial officials liked to call it, that the image of Bali became firmly entrenched both in popular descriptions and in scholarly works. The 1920's and 1930's in particular were years in which a variety of experts in the fields of anthropology, linguistics, archaeology and religion came to work in Bali and developed an elaborate and respectable portrait of the island as a sort of "Last Paradise," even when they saw evidence to the contrary.

The Dutch had formally taken control of the island in 1908 after decades of failed invasions and partial victories against Bali's indigenous rajas, or kings. The first tourists soon arrived on the Dutch steamship line, sailing from Suez in boats like the *Cingalese Princess*.

But the new overlords were confronted with a dilemma. After the First World War, the influences of nationalism and communism began to be felt. The Dutch did not want to involve themselves in yet more bloody repressions—a more sane modus operandi, to their mind, was the reinstallation of the deposed native royal families and ruling classes.

They therefore devised a thing called the Ethical Policy, which could be roughly interpreted as a commitment to preserve the heritage of the people they were ruling against their wills. It had its roots in the nineteenth century and in European scholars who had settled in Bali to study its Hinduism and its ancient scripts. The first of these, curiously enough, was the same Warren Hastings who had created Calcutta—he was given stewardship of Bali between 1811 and 1818. As in Calcutta, Hastings thought to revive Hindu learning;

as in India, the idea of the romantic village was quick to take hold. He was followed by an eccentric band of Orientalists—misfits like Baron Wolter van Hoëvell, the wandering alcoholic Mads Lange, and the doctor Julius Jacobs, who first "discovered" a Bali of picturesque dancing girls and male whores.

These scholars—the Ethici, as they were known—soon came to think that Bali was a kind of fossilized remain of the older Hindu culture of neighboring Java, which had since fallen under the regrettable sway of a more modern Islam. It was therefore a precious time capsule, a museum of antiquities that had to be saved from oblivion. This was true not just of its artifacts and its scriptures written in Kawi, the ancient language of Java, but of all aspects of its ritual and mythological life. Friedrich Liefrinck extolled the virtues of the pure Balinese village, an idea that later convinced the Dutch that it had to be restored.

In the period between the two great world wars, the Dutch gathered up the visions of the Ethici and turned them into a political policy of sorts, regrouping the scattered rajas and their families and relegalizing the caste system. This recreation of tradition, which was not necessarily tradition at all, served to reassert a conservative social order that could better resist the inroads of aggressive modern ideologies from more restless Java. The photography of the '20s is awash with gorgeously attired royal families—many of them looking like stunned deer in the proverbial headlights—bare-breasted dancing girls and restored temples, a Bali remade as exotic, ancient, and timeless. This was the Dutch colonial artifice, and an essential part of its script was the notion of a unique island that was both outside history and unscarred by its violent conflicts. Bali was the eternal village: folklore, witches, trances, sexuality, and art.

Dutch power was able to maintain this fantasy until the Japanese came storming up Sanur beach in 1942. The Dutch came back in 1946, but they immediately became embroiled in the National Revolution of 1945–49. It has been largely written out of Bali's image, but thousands died on the island during the struggles to define Indonesian independence—though the bloodshed was nothing compared to the massacres that were in store for Bali in the 1960s.

Indonesia's first president, the fantastical, sinister Sukarno, quickly discovered what the Dutch had: that Bali could serve as a symbolic cornerstone of conservative "Javanese" tradition within the chaotic tapestry of a vast, shambling nation made up of hundreds of ethnicities, religions, and separatist aspirations. As such, it had to be balmy and peaceable; outside the fray, as it were. The Island of Culture created in the '30s was resurrected in the 1950s as Sukarno feted state guests at his Bali palace. But Sukarno played both sides of the coin—he patronized Ubud while encouraging the grimly radical Governor Suteja to keep the revolution burning. At the same time, he sent Bali's dance troupes around the world, including the famed dancer I Nyoman Kakul, who was immortalized by Cartier-Bresson.

Only the abortive coup in 1965 and the following anticommunist bloodbath interrupted the progress of Bali's revived career as a showcase of ancient tradition and folklorish stability. At the end of 1965, armed gangs roamed the island, mutilating and beheading their victims; the hallowed villages vaunted by anthropologists for their peacefulness and charm elected execution squads to carry out collective murders.

It is amazing to see how powerfully the tourist brochures of the Dutch period have stamped upon Bali an image that even the Balinese have adopted. Back in 1946, a Dutch military adviser had expressed the image quite neatly:

> The Balinese is a remarkable Oriental. He is very artistic, and expresses this in music, dance, wood carving and silver work. Although he is a poor fighter, because he is cowardly, the Balinese is self-confident and therefore very free in his association with others, including Europeans, though he does this in a pleasant way. He is good-humored and likes to join in a good joke. These character traits are certainly part of the reason for the great success of tourism here. (Captain J. B. T. Konig, quoted in Robinson, *The Dark Side of Paradise*).

But the American poet Frederick Seidel, writing of the 1965 massacres in his poem "Bali," gives voice to the other side of the coin:

> *Gentle Balinese murdered gentle Balinese,*
> *And, in the usual pogrom, killed*
> *The smart hardworking Chinese,*
> *Merchants to the poor, Jews in paradise.*

The Santika Garden hotel was only a few hundred yards up the hill of Jalan Raya from Walter Spies's legendary villa, now converted into the Tjampuhan Hotel. I could walk there every morning before the rain came down. There were two ways to get there. The main road took one directly to the gates, but there was also a secretive shortcut across a rocky river sunk deep below the main road. Spies had built his house at the confluence of two small rivers that the Balinese consider to be magically charged, and above a small temple. The path is a series of steep steps cut into the hillside, with pavilions perched on the edge of countless terraces and a pool set inside a wedge of jungle. Spies's own house is still here. Though very few of his paintings are housed within it, his carved monkeys still emerge out of the long walls. It is a few minutes before you realize that the whole thing is a fantasy of the 1930s, like the set of the Bob Hope movie *The Road to Bali*. You expect Dorothy Lamour to come padding out to the pool in a priestess hat. The bohemians are gone, and there is no memory of Margaret Mead and Gregory Bateson, Jane Belo, or her musicologist husband Colin McPhee, the glittering crowd that hatched our idea of Bali when Kuta was still an empty beach. In her *Letters*, Mead describes coming to this house in April 1936 only a few hours after arriving in Bali on the Dutch ship *Tapaneoli* from Singapore. She was enchanted from the moment she landed, driving across island landscapes that seemed to her remarkably dense, compacted, and rich:

> It is the most extraordinary combination of a relatively untouched native life going along smoothly and quietly in its old way with a kind of extraneous, external civilization superimposed like an extra nervous system put on the outside of a body. Motor roads of black loose stones run through villages which are each protected by a magic wall against demons and over the heads of the motorists a screen of pointed bamboo is aimed at the demons.

Spies was to be Mead's mentor, her guiding spirit in Bali. "Walter is a perfectly delightful person," she wrote, "an artist and a musician who has lived in Bali for some eight years." A wealthy aristocrat born in Russia in 1895 to a Dresden family, Spies had arrived in Bali in 1927 after having worked as a court musician for the sultan of Yogyakarta in Java. He was a close friend of Friedrich Murnau, director of the 1922 *Nosferatu*, and Murnau's chiaroscuro techniques can be seen in Spies's paintings of Bali's demonic rites. He became both a fervent photographer of Balinese life and a collector of folktales, music, and artifacts; his idealization of the Balinese peasant, meanwhile, harked back consciously to the Ethici.

Magic and the village: Spies's influence on Mead is obvious. But he was also a driving force behind the globalizing—if we can call it that—of Bali's image. Vickers describes how at the 1931 Colonial Exhibition in Paris, Spies shaped the Balinese exhibition. (It was where Antonin Artaud saw his first Balinese dance, a fierce influence on his "theater of cruelty.") A book of Spies's Bali photographs was also a sensation, and soon the smart set was paying house calls in Ubud. He also contributed to André Roosevelt's film about Bali, *Goona Goona*, which made that phrase ("love magic" in Javanese) a part of '20s New York slang. Later, he made a great impression upon the wandering Mexican caricaturist Miguel Covarrubias, author of perhaps the most read book about Bali, the 1937 *Island of Bali*. The tone is already utopian. "Like a continual under-sea ballet," Covarrubias writes, "the pulse of life in Bali moves with a measured rhythm . . . no other race gives the impression of living in such close touch with nature, creates such a complete feeling of harmony between the people and their surroundings."

Spies, Mead, and Covarrubias helped refine an idea that has not died since. Their reasons for being here were all different, however. Spies came to Bali in no small part because it was easier to be a homosexual, but during a 1939 witch hunt that swept through the Dutch Indies he was tried and imprisoned. Shipped out of Bali as an undesirable alien at the height of the Pacific war, he was drowned when his prison ship was bombed in 1942. The cells were not unlocked as the ship went down.

Mead, on the other hand, had been sent to Bali for a curiously specific purpose—to investigate the cultural roots of schizophrenia for the fearsomely named Committee for Research in Dementia Praecox. Bali had seemed to her a fertile place to research such a thing. Repression, she theorized, made the Balinese very susceptible to forms of schizophrenia. Over a period of two years, she and Bateson devised a new method of research using film, photography, and text accounts, and a desire to compare their results with another subject area led them to think about comparative research in Papua. Bali, then, led to Papua.

Under the influence of Spies, one suspects, Mead and Belo became obsessed with the Rangda witch dance and its accompanying trances. The altered state of trance could be analyzed from different angles, its roots in the Balinese psyche could be conjectured with great finesse. But Mead's interests reinforced a conception of the Balinese as an archaic and static people with no real history to them. There was much talk of a "steady state" and an unchanging but dynamic harmony. "Here the ahistorical nature of anthropology," writes Vickers, "relegated non-Europeans to being people without history."

Mead's letters from her adopted village of Bojong Gede crackle with the freshness of unexpected discovery. It is a traveler's pleasure. Perhaps an anthropologist has to be a good traveler *first*. But as I walked around the Spies house I thought back to the exhibits in the airport and the nauseatingly ubiquitous gamelan music in the phony artisan shops all over Ubud. Bali was not unchanging or harmonious. Its depth had been flattened out, its demonic edges funneled into spectacles, and this had happened not in spite of the serious traveler and the serious anthropologist, but because of them.

It rains all the time in Ubud in November. I could no longer train with the pack, so I spent hours trudging up and down Monkey Forest Road, all the way down to the Monkey Forest itself, past a slew of empty luxury hotels and open bars where, between eleven and midnight, little crowds of foreigners gathered to watch jazz bands and R & B outfits. The rain turned the football field into a marsh. At night, the temples lit up and the dances went on as always; along Raya, the boutiques filled with *krisses* and scabbards, handmade quilts and shadow puppets stood like stores in New York or Paris along the high sidewalks, but bestilled and perceptibly melancholy. Sellers have finally outstripped buyers to such a degree that a polite desperation has set in. Every store is stuffed with artisanal merchandise, much of it excellent, but no one will ever buy so much replicated authenticity dragged from the past, or from an idea of the past. I remembered Mead's account of a young peasant who came to her house one day trying to sell a badly made sculpture. After she had given him some tips as to how to improve his technique—a technique that as a Balinese he might have been expected to know better than she—he came back almost every day thereafter with his gradually improving product. Even when she clearly had no intention of buying anything, he came. He came because it was a hope, or else because it was something to do, and because it was a contact with a foreigner and contact with a foreigner is always interestingly unpredictable. The same kind of contact happens by the minute in Ubud. The whole town is a theme park based on a version of Bali that Europeans invented, but inside the park two peoples still tried to make something mutually lucrative happen. The old conceit of coming to Ubud for spirituality had clearly worn thin; the Westerners no longer really believed in it. I had the impression that the Balinese too no longer believed in what they were selling. The monkey dances—the *kecak*—the "peace and tranquility," the sublime vistas of rice paddies fading into misty hillsides—it was no longer life.

The traveler always reaches a point where, fixed in a place for a while, he asks himself why he is there. Ubud has the prettiest hotels in the world. Between them, the paddies opened up like ancient ponds, sleepy under the rain, and there were long moments when I could have stayed there for months on end. But it was no longer life. At the Tutmak, we began plotting Papua, looking at maps, comparing malaria treatments, watching the clocks as if counting down. The other three Europeans joining the trip would soon be flying into Denpasar. It was like a reality show game: we would meet them only at the airport at two a.m. on the morning we were due to fly out to Jayapura. Flights to Papua always fly out in the middle of the night. It is because there is no demand for them and because most of the passengers are going to Papua for business. The gold mine in Timika, the natural gas companies in the capital. It is curious to see: the hordes of tourists gathering to fly off to Bangkok on one side of the facility, and on the other side the dozen or so anxious lost souls gathered in a shabby little side terminal to get on board our three a.m. flight.

There were a few Indonesians of the earnest variety, clutching threadbare suitcases and smoking intensely in the heat outside. From the parking lot, the three Europeans suddenly arrived, looking incredibly fresh, white, and eager. They were already in jungle gear. The Indonesian cops stared.

Georg Decristoforo and Theresia Ellinger, a couple in their fifties from the Austrian Tyrol, and a young blond Finn named Juha. They were all three scientists. Georg and Theresia were chemical engineers with the Sandoz pharmaceutical company, a subsidiary of Novartis; Juha designed software for the European Space Agency with a small company outside Helsinki.

I looked them over one by one. Georg: the classic image of a German scientist. Dark cropped hair, midfifties, spectacles, uncomplaining enthusiasm. I thought of the entomologist in Kobe Abe's *Woman in the Dunes*. He alone had brought a GPS device, the latest jungle camping gadgets, high-tech timekeeping machines. He ate everything—taro chips, hot chocolate, tempeh—like a merry vacuum cleaner, smacking his lips and regaling the table with exotic scientific factoids. No disgust, no quease. His lover, Theresia: the classic image of an English public school matron, sturdy and intolerant of nonsense, ruddy high Alpine cheekbones and powerful hands that knew how to tie complicated nautical knots or tent lines. The formidable widow in *Woman in the Dunes*.

All three were amiable. No cranks, no psychopaths here. They had been carefully screened. I asked Theresia what her favorite pastime was. *"Vinter mountaineering!"* That, and trekking in Nepal.

Juha was more my age. I quickly understood that he and I were the novices. While Georg and Theresia roamed the planet looking for difficult environments in which to hone their formidable wilderness skills, we lived soft lives. Juha seemed like a romantic engineer, if one can imagine such a thing, but with almost white Nordic eyes suggesting a perpetual question mark, an unmodern irony.

There are conversations between strangers whose content has nothing to do with their purpose. We must have been there for roughly similar reasons, driven by comparable discontents, and so what we said to each other did not matter very much. Just arrived from Europe, the others were feeling the heat. They were tense, apprehensive. Meanwhile, something had quietly snapped inside me, a bond connecting me to the comfortable infrastructure of travel itself, or else to the hopes that always hover around a voyage. It is in airports, in any case, that I always make a final reckoning with the life I have lived up till then as well as the unknown place that I am about to enter. If, like me, you think you are going to die every time you fly, you do this—it is like saying the Last Rites to yourself.

Beyond the shabby glass doors lay the airport car park. Its anonymity appeared far more obvious than it had been two hours earlier. The Trigana propeller plane was already there and it had a frayed look about it, like a dog that has seen too many winters. Rain beat on the wings and the flight was delayed for three hours. In the waiting room, a Papuan sat smoking pencil-thin cigars, his brown suit clashing with a pair of trainers and a large gold ring. He stared through the windows for hours and did not move a muscle. Eventually, we too fell into morose silence. For the last hour no one spoke a word.

THE NAKED TOURIST

For centuries, Europeans and their offshoots have searched for hidden valleys, lost kingdoms, vanished islands, and sunken civilizations. I don't know whether the Japanese or the Indians share such obsessions and travel in order to exorcize them. But if they do not, and the pathology is indeed unique, then I assume that something about us is proved. After El Dorado and Atlantis, for example, there was Shangri-La, supposedly a Tibetan word for paradise. It entered the vocabulary of English in 1933 when the British writer James Hilton published a novel called *Lost Horizon*. Hilton invented an isolated Himalayan kingdom of unsullied peace and harmony into which a band of Westerners stumble after surviving an air crash. Hilton's vision inspired President Franklin Roosevelt to name what is now Camp David "Shangri-La."

But Hilton was careful to add that the path to Shangri-La could not be retraced, nor its location found on any map. Hilton himself never visited China or Tibet and seems to have made the place up, but that has not stopped China from recently declaring the invention of a new "ecological tourist region" to be called "Shangrila," a denomination long hotly contested by two miserable Chinese cities, Zhongdian and Deqen. Whichever place gets to call itself Shangrila is assured a windfall of tourist dollars; people will flock there, drawn simply by the name. It would be like a tiny municipality in the Amazon being called El Dorado.

How strange that a notion achieved purely in the realm of religious ideas should translate itself into real geography. It is like those medieval maps that coolly indicate "Eden" as lying somewhere between the Tigris and the Euphrates rivers. Just as pilgrims made their way to a postage-stamp-sized garden called Gethsemane—but with the difference that Eden existed outside the mythical histories that give the world its various shrines. The physical visiting of something that exists only inside the realm of ideas—is this a Western folly?

It is certainly Christian. The Greeks had their Garden of Hesperides located tantalizingly just beyond the Pillars of Hercules, and therefore out of reach. But only Christians had Eden as a place of primordial innocence, an innocence to which we must return. By now, it is hardwired into us.

Every travel book employs the insidious device of the writer peering down through his airplane window and seeing this or that land, which is always made to look otherworldly. I have flown into hundreds of cities and countries, looked down through a thousand porthole windows to see surprising vistas hurtling toward me out of the mists. But only flying into Timika did I feel a *continual* unease. Papua is almost always shrouded in clouds. Its soaring mountains rise out of the sea, the forests seeping down to the rivers where there is nothing, just fingers of sand and a color of stewed tea. You fly over fogs, under which the tops of trees move in horrifying slow motion. Along a valley there is a little road, visible between rolling mists, and on the road there is a man walking; you see him, even from the air, and you see his dog ahead of him.

Near Timika lies the world's largest gold mine, the sinister Freeport. It is a violent place, cordoned off. Two Americans were killed here a little while back. The rumor is that the Indonesian military staged an attack to discredit the Papuan independents. No one can enter there unless he is employed by the Anglo-American mining company. While the plane is refueling, if you are continuing on, you are not allowed off it. A few armed men sit under the perimeter palms, staring sullenly at the plane. An American gets off, his back drenched with sweat even at dawn. A few Indonesians board and soon we number about fifteen. I notice that everyone looks each other over rather carefully. There are no women, apart from Theresia.

After two hours in Timika, we went on to Sentani, the suburb of Jayapura that houses its tiny airport. The skies cleared. Thousands of palms clustered around headlands and coves and clearings at the top of the hills. Jayapura is actually built around islets and islands, straddling the sea. It's an Indonesian city with minarets and traffic jams, but few outside of Papua and the shantytowns of Java are much aware of its existence. The immigrants here are Javanese, beneficiaries of the UN-sponsored "transmigration program" that has dispersed millions of settlers from overcrowded Java around the rest of Indonesia. An old Dutch quarter manages to survive.

At Sentani, the mood is different, for the mountains come much closer and only one bedraggled highway runs along their base. It is Papuan, not Javan. The iconography here is

Christian and pagan; huge white crosses dominate the hillsides. There is no sign even of a city.

The airport is flanked by towering tribal totems and sculptures. You must walk across the airstrip toward the soft green mountains that tower above it, the heat already shot through with a smell of petrol and fragrant mud. Inside the terminal, there is the faint scent of a different humanity, the Papuans crowded around to gawp at the aliens coming off the runway. They are dressed, but some wear chicken feathers in their hair. They watch you with a cool, unmoved fixation, as if you were a walking traffic accident covered with your own blood. These are urban Papuans, runaways from the dark interior. Walking into this terminal I felt like Lévi-Strauss contemplating the deck of his first ship into the tropics:

> Over and above those heroes—navigators, explorers and conquerors of the New World—who (before the era of journeys to the moon) undertook the only total adventure open to man, my thoughts turn to the survivors of a rearguard which paid so cruelly for the honour of keeping the gates wide open. I mean the Indians, whose example, through Montaigne, Rousseau, Voltaire and Diderot, enriched the substance of what I was taught at school. Hurons, Iroquois, Caribs and Tupi—I was now on my way to them!

I called it the Blue Hotel, and perhaps it was the only one in Sentani. It stood on a side street among flowering gardens, in the shadow of the mountains. Here we had to wait while

Woolford extracted our permits for travel into the interior from a reluctant and corrupt police authority in Jayapura. The place was blue throughout; the spartan rooms had buckets in the bathrooms, no running water, and cots for beds. It rained ceaselessly, and the banana trees rocked gently up and down like handheld fans.

A Russian air crew flying cargo planes sat down every night to their own table, laid with Bulgarian jams and chilled butter. It was rumored they brought Papuan whores back to the $4 rooms. Salesmen from Papua New Guinea in cheap suits munched their toast in the restaurant where the TV played a dubbed *Life of Chopin* over and over. In the corridor outside, frogs sang in a small pool filled with half-dead fish. Sometimes it was the only sound, the frogs rasping with the rain. The salesmen watched the tortures of Chopin on Mallorca with George Sand with steady but utterly empty eyes. Extraterrestrials, white men, pianists.

During the day, I read or walked around the mud streets, taking photographs of the gardens. Come sundown, it was time to go to Sentani's only halfway salubrious restaurant, Mickey's. Sentani is where Papuans and Javans mix uneasily. Its streets are trash and pools; candles set on tables of betel nuts serve as streetlights. The sidewalks are spattered with great bright red pools of spittled betel juice. When the Papuans drink a few beers, they totter along with a hint of belligerence, their eyes bulging.

At Mickey's, the Russians also had their special table. Each time they came in, swaggering in their airline caps and T-shirts, I wondered to myself why white men are so unable to dress in our age. How much more elegant the Korowai men looked in the few photographs I had seen, naked but for a penis-sheathing acorn or hornbill bill—Papuans call their penis gourds *kotekas*, and it is often their sole item of fashion. How much better dressed. The Russians glared around them. A badly dressed man glaring is a scary item. Occasionally, a Papuan walked by, hair alive with chicken feathers. But no bow, no arrows. The forest has been banished from Sentani. These Papuans are tamed, reduced to a predictable urban paupery.

One morning, we drove into Jayapura along a winding road that hugs the edge of a vast lake. There were houses raised on stilts above the water, more giant white crosses, an abandoned hotel that must once have catered to the PNG salesmen crowd. But then you are suddenly in the city, which is Muslim, minareted, tense with uncertain moods. The border of PNG is only a few miles along the coast; Al Qaeda does a lot of cross-border traffic in drugs and weapons. Yet Jayapura itself is unexpectedly pleasant: a breezy Dutch city built around and over a series of steep hills. It is filled with Papuan markets, where you can buy masks and *kotekas*. The coffee shops are large and lurid, and filled with brooding young men with nothing to do. It was here, however, that our little band began to coalesce. As I had suspected, our motives were not dissimilar—I think I could say that in each case it was a desire to get out of the known world, and we all have our private worlds that are all too known. What lies beyond it? Is there a beyond at all?

On the one-hour flight to Wamena, you notice that there are no roads into this interior; the plane rises above glaciers and volcanic ridges—Mount Carstensz here is the seventh tallest peak in the world. Some of the peaks are almost at the same height as the plane, snarling spirelights obscured by whorls of mist. The plane shudders and rocks. A Götterdämmerung panorama opens up, the heads of volcanoes suddenly appearing through banks of tinted mist, and far below valleys as intensely green as pond alga, bordered with walls of ice.

The first aviators who ventured here in the 1940s were the first non-Papuans, as far as we are aware, to penetrate into the Baliem, which might as well have been renamed the Lost Valley—for rarely has an actual place conformed so startlingly to a cultural fantasy. The Kremer expedition had reached the lower levels of the Snow Mountains in 1921 but had been forced to abandon its biological specimens. Richard Archbold, the Baliem's official "discoverer," was a mammalogist and private millionaire working for the American Museum of Natural History who flew this same path in a huge Catalina seaplane christened the *Guba*—the same plane that had been modified by Howard Hughes for salmon expeditions in Alaska. His discovery of the Baliem was a total surprise. He saw the Dani watchtowers, the prehistoric terraces, the river snaking through the valley's bottom, and his report prompted the Dutch to send a small military expedition to the two nearby alpine lakes of Habbemaat and Meervlakte, with Archbold assisting. Fifty-six Dutch officers and men and seventy-three Dayak porters from Borneo were accompanied by thirty convicts—the Archbold Expedition, as it is known, was to study the area between Mount Wilhelmina to the south and the Taritatu River to the north. Leaving from the two base camps at Lake Habbemaat and the Taritatu, two patrols were to meet up in the Baliem Valley.

The Dani greeted the patrols amicably. As they approached the Baliem, however, the situation grew tense. At one point, the Dutch encountered a war party; two Dani were shot dead. No explanation for the sudden hostility is given in the official Dutch account. The latter was more concerned with frostbite and altitude sickness. The two patrols met up in the Baliem without incident; at a welcome feast in their honor, the Dani sprinkled the Europeans and Americans with pig blood.

The Dutch journals record the extensive nature of Dani agriculture. Using timbered and stone terraces and crop rotation, they raised sweet potatoes, cucumbers, sugarcane, tobacco, bananas, spinach, and beans. The expedition introduced peanuts, which were soon wildly popular. Cowrie shells were used as currency—ten good ones bought a pig. The expedition lasted fourteen months and produced a *National Geographic* article that caused a sensation back in the United States. But the moment of "firstness" is very short-lived, maybe only a matter of minutes. The Baliem Valley entered the tourist economy in the following decades, modestly, it is true, but irrevocably. A resort was even built by a German tour operator high up on one of its mountainsides. It is mostly empty now, as Papua's reputation for violence drove Europeans elsewhere, but there were still a few takers from season to season. The "Stone Age," meanwhile, had receded to the far side of another range of impassable mountains, to the south.

The plane slips between black and purple peaks as it descends into Wamena, an alpine land as wet and mossy as Scotland. The terraces are still there, and the river still shines over beds of pebbles, flanked with fenced gardens of taro.

The Dani huts are connected by long paths along which mo-torcycles and bikes glitter when the sun comes out. The air smells of snow and pastures, the sweet odor of grass; by the runway, naked men stand glistening with pig fat, shivering in the mist and holding out fossilized toadstools for sale.

As we walked the four blocks from the tiny airport to the Hotel Renggku, four or five of them followed us with their toadstools, dog-tooth necklaces, and breastplates of sewn cowrie shells. They all wore tall *kotekas* decorated with tufts of pig fur that they shook with one hand, expressing a gesture that is said to mean something like "Wow!" They walked on wide, flat feet, the biggest feet I had ever seen. (The Dani make formidable soccer players.) The pig fat gave them a sweet, peculiar odor and they passed their palms across ours as they murmured, in high nasal tones, "*Wa wa wa*"—welcome, hello, how are you? It was a hustle, but a mild one. At the hotel they simply parked themselves outside the front door and stayed there for three days.

The Renggku was run by Christian Indonesians. The electricity was off and there had probably never been running water. There was a large photomural of a New England forest turning color, all gold and scarlet, and a Christmas tree stood in a corner of the dining room, its lights ready to go on when the juice returned. The Papuans wandered in and out as if unwilling to recognize the concept of doors. They sat on the sofa of the lobby and twanged away at small bamboo harps. If you caught their eye they would stop twanging for a moment, bare betel-red teeth, and sing *wa wa wa*. They sometimes crowded around the water fountain and its pile of small paper cups, silently watching the bubbles. It was quite cold and they never stopped shivering; the rain was getting heavier and all around us the mountains were cloaked in clouds.

I went into my room and lay down, exhausted already for some reason. It was the Muslim holiday of Idul Fitri and the muezzins began to wail, although there are hardly any Muslims in Wamena and the Dani are a pig-worshipping culture. I thought back to Hamza Mustafa's words about the Indonesians building a new Islamic university in Wamena with Saudi money. It seemed an impossible provocation. Just after our arrival, we heard a rumor over cups of Nescafé that twelve Indonesian soldiers had been killed the day before by Papuans armed with bows and arrows, a few miles out of town. It was difficult to say if it was true, but it was certainly the case that Papuans had recently stormed the police HQ and killed many Indonesians with arrows. The mutual suspicion was intense enough to be noticeable even to a foreigner. I could hear it in the muezzins, somehow, shrieking through the dark as the Dani in the lobby lit up their pipes and scowled.

I was asleep when Chief Yali woke me up. He came in just to say hello, and when I opened my eyes from nightmares I saw a perfect Orientalist fantasy: a delicate naked man covered in pig fat dancing by my bed, a lofty carrot-shaped wooden penis gourd tied to his head with a piece of string. He kissed my hand. The electricity was now down all over Wamena and the town was plunged in total darkness. But muezzins still sang, the rain still struck the tin roofs. As lightning shot through the broken windows, Yali swung his little hips back and forth and giggled all the same: it was dinnertime. Rising wearily, I uttered the only Dani phrase I had mastered so far. *Wa wa wa.*

"*Wa,*" he said. His face was smeared with shiny black paint and his arms were spotted with white clay.

Woolford is Yali's adopted son. The American has been coming to Wamena for sixteen years, and they kissed as father and son. Although Woolford does not speak any Dani, Yali has learned a little Bahasa Indonesian. The table was set with fried tempeh and plates of sautéed taro, a beautifully wild purple color. The table was lit with candles, and into their orbit came wild-eyed men floating in from the darkness wearing dog-tooth necklaces. Boys in pig fur hats twanged on bamboo harps as the doorways dripped and the thunder rolled. And there was William, Kelly's right-hand man, and Penus, who was going to be our cook in the jungle. Kelly introduced him to us.

"Hello, Penus," Theresia and Georg said, shaking his hand.

Penus well understood the jolly double entendre.

His laugh was like that of the Jolly Green Giant, setting Yali in motion again like some clockwork toy. Dancing, dancing, the hips jigging. Waltzes in the dark, *wa wa wa*.

"Are they always naked," Juha asked mildly, looking at the naked Dani grinning back at us, "or do they only take their clothes off for us?"

Whether or not they preferred nakedness, it was more elegant than wearing Nike T-shirts.

"Are they cold?" Theresia asked. "Is that why they're covered with pig fat?"

"Cold," Yali suddenly said in English. "Good cold. *Wa.*"

"He speaks a little English?" Juha asked.

A few tourists had already gone to his compound near the village of Akima to see the three-hundred-year-old mummy of the great warrior Werapak Elosarek.

Penus cut us some pineapples. He spoke quite reasonable English from his years of working with Woolford.

"Yali is famous. He has been in the magazines. He is the Dani everyone know."

The old geezer had a canny look in his eye. He sidled up and laid his cheek against the back of my hand. "Me love you here."

We ate with the Papuans staring at us by candlelight, crowded round like spectators at a circus atrocity, and indeed they shivered; the goose bumps on their skin were visible. We wore sweaters. Afterward, I wandered outside, restless, a little claustrophobic, and thirsty. The hotel owners said there was a small store down the street where I could buy some plastic bags of orange drink. I set off, though with some misgiving. Wamena's streets at night are only reasonably safe. There are no streetlights, and away from the larger houses and the airport the gloom is dense. Two blocks away I was lost, stumbling from corner to corner. Warriors wrapped in blankets padded past hand in hand, soaked from the rain, their bodies shiny, as if soaped. Bicycle rickshaws rattled past. Seeing me, the haunted-looking boys did a sharp U-turn and came up, tossing a few words of Bahasa at me. Eventually, feeling alarmed and drained by the wet, I took one to the main market a few blocks distant, which was alive and kicking at eight p.m. So the juice had come back on. Not knowing where to be let off, I waited till we reached a cake shop and stopped there. Two Javan women were serving milk coffee and lemon cakes under a few red bulbs. I dove in and sat by a window with no glass. The whole street was awash with farm implements flown in from the coast—spades, flashlights, plastic buckets, blankets, tarpaulins, hoes, rakes, axes. Among these were scattered Javan shops filled with DVDs and cassettes. The rain had turned the street to four inches of mud, and through it slogged desperate-looking men in ragged shorts, heavily muscled and carrying axes. The eyes emitted a wild flash as they scanned the shops. I thought, Please don't see me. Eventually I was seen, and a tall old man with bark earrings lunged through the flap door armed with a huge greasy machete. He staggered into the cake shop as if tipsy and stared at me with pop eyes. The Javan women began arguing with him, and I think the word they kept repeating meant "Out!" The madman pointed at me. Raindrops dripped from his nose and from hair sprinkled with wet feathers. He seemed disoriented more than anything. When he had been evicted, the Javans served me more coffee. They looked at me with nervous pity.

How many times in the course of a life do you think you are searching out "the other"? But when the real thing is staring you in the face—without any mediation of superior force from your own civilization—a brutal shock takes hold of you. All your atavistic feelings of fear, insecurity, and tribal chauvinism return to the fore of your consciousness, dragged out from the obscure sediment where they have been languishing since enlightened schoolteachers sent them to the bottom of your psyche all those years ago. They stir; adrenaline pumps through your soul. The sanctimonious reflex of the anthropologist will not help you. It is rare even to be in a place where not a single word of the so-called global language is spoken. Where the tourist infrastructure does not exist.

I got a rickshaw home, but it left me at the wrong block. I had to walk, lost yet again. Reaching a particularly obscure corner where the rain had reached a new crescendo, I stopped to get my bearings. A small hand suddenly slipped into mine and, controlling myself, I didn't cry out. Looking down, I found that I had been "seized" by a tiny man about three or four feet tall. It was a Yali pygmy, a tribe from higher up the valley, and his *koteka* was taller than his own head. A high-pitched voice came out from a pair of white eyes. *Wa wa wa!* Without saying a word, he took me back to the Renggku for a packet of tobacco. It was like being led by a fairy child—and I the huge buffoon who has wandered into the wrong tale.

The next day, our group drove out to Yali's compound for a traditional pig feast. A small metal road took us through the fertile, flat fields of the valley bottom, thick with peanut trees and tubby black pigs. On the way we stopped at a pig fair, held in an open space next to the food market. The men came up quickly, urgently—buy a pig? They could not comprehend the refusal. We were clearly rich yet did not want a pig. Madness. Pure obstinacy.

The day was misty and wet, the paths to the compound churned to a heavy, tiring mud. The warriors put on a battle for us, chasing about under the Scottish hills with their spears, arrayed in red feathers. And there was Yali in a tree-like lookout post pretending to shoot arrows at us. But the whole thing was a preplanned show. The smooth seven-foot spears had not drawn blood in a while.

Inside the compound the pigs were chased around and then shot with wedge-shaped arrows. The carcasses were roasted on hot stones smothered with piles of leaves; awaiting the results, the men retired to their lodge, a smoky cabin festooned with pig jaws where we smoked in near-total darkness. I couldn't help thinking that eventually it must always occur to an indigenous people that their primitivity is what is most valuable about them in the eyes of outsiders. Primitivity—always naked and in feathers—is the one economic asset they possess. As soon as they put on T-shirts and sneakers, they cease to be of any value—even though the Korowai and Kombai, I had heard, love Western clothes and wear them whenever they can.

At some point, I naïvely asked Yali if he knew anything about the outside world, and a cowering, doglike resentment flashed across his face. Yali had been taken to Japan the year before by a Balinese businessman and his Japanese wife. It had been a sorry affair. Paraded around Japan like the Elephant Man, Yali had been dumped on a plane to Jakarta with no money and then left to beg his way home.

The men began to sing their songs, which were mournful rather than merry. The room filled with smoke. Yali asked me questions. Did I have a house with dogs? Hearing that I had not one dog, he shook his head. Ah, sad man, sad man. Coughing and blackened with smoke, we reemerged into the rain. They all seemed bronchitic, as bronchitic as I am myself. They smoked more than the French.

On the way back, we stopped at Akima to see the

mummy of Werapak Elosarek. The village is a sea of mud, a long enclosure walled in with thatch huts. The mummy is wheeled out by a grumpy old man and sat on a tree stump. A group of well-heeled tourists from Jakarta suddenly came in, the women shrieking with disgust at the mud and the smell of pig shit. They peered aghast at the naked women chewing on sweet potatoes. Then they took their pictures of the mummy, which was curled in a fetal position on his stump. The flashes competed drearily with the lightning overhead and suddenly I wanted to escape. Poor old Werapak. How could a king of seventeenth-century Papua have ever imagined ending up as a photogenic spectacle on a tree stump? But then, how could Yali have ever imagined being stranded in Narita airport? It is easy to say that the world is a strange place, but the more you contemplate that strangeness, the more you are enraged.

Before dawn, we were at the airstrip. The Seventh-Day Adventist Pilatus plane arrived, and a Christian captain in a white uniform supervised the filling of the fuel tanks amid a group of Papuans. The fuel was cranked by hand through a hose pipe. He came up and shook our hands. The Adventists fly to the Yanimura and do not ordinarily stop at Wanggemalo, now that the missionaries are gone. So this was going to be an exception, an exception that would cost us handsomely.

"So you're off to Wanggemalo, eh?"

He might as well have added, "Poor bastards."

"Quite a fun place," he did add. But he winked at the same time. I went for a walk with Juha.

"He seems very amused," I observed.

"He knows something we don't."

But the sun had come out, the hills looked as if they were cloaked in flowering gorse. The shadows of clouds raced across them. Naked men sauntered nonchalantly across the grass runway.

"I don't care if he does. I *prefer* that he does. It's what we signed up for," Juha admitted. "It's what we are after. I am just not sure what that is. I thought of getting out of Finland, away from my wife for a little while—and I hate vacations."

"I hate vacations, too."

"I am not even sure that I like traveling."

And of course that was it in a nutshell.

The immense pile of equipment about to be loaded onto the plane begged the question whether this qualified as "travel." It was what saved us from complete banality. And yet—

"I keep thinking about the Dani," I said. "And about yesterday with Chief Yali. I kept thinking that he was an impostor, and then that he couldn't possibly be an impostor. Because *I* am the impostor here."

"Yes, we are impostors, of course."

I said, "He *felt* like a strange one. Was he a touristic creation?"

"No. But I see what you mean. We are out of our depth."

"But he wasn't an impostor, was he?"

For what is an impostor on Planet Tourism, anyway?

Juha's calm blue eyes surveyed the naked men on the runway. A *scene*. But of what? The Dani were too picturesque by half. But the Kombai were going to be a very different matter.

As we were loading the plane with the aforementioned provisions—sacks of rice, boxes of peanut butter, biscuits, noodles—Kelly elaborated his own ideas of the matter at hand: "We're going to find Kombai who have never even *heard* of white people, let alone seen any. You'll see that look in their eyes."

That look?

"Yeah, that look. We're flying to the most godforsaken place on earth. Compared to Wanggemalo, Wamena is like Manhattan."

We looked back at the perimeter fence and saw the same naked pygmy from the Yali tribe standing in the sunlight with his huge *koteka*, smiling in forlornly. *Wa wa wa*, he cried, waving.

"Like *The Lost World*?" I said. And I added that Arthur Conan Doyle had once suggested Papua New Guinea as a new Jewish homeland.

"What a nut," Woolford drawled. "I guess he never went to Wanggemalo."

But perhaps, I thought, that was precisely the point.

ANYWHERE OUT OF THE WORLD

With the doors open, we flew over the glaciers that separate Wamena from the Merauke forests. Beyond the mountains, the plane drops quite suddenly and you are skimming across the roof of a forest that stretches from horizon to horizon: the largest primary forest in the world after the Amazon. It is a hypnotic voyage. You soon lose all bearings as the volcanoes disappear and your eyes seem to fill with a psychological greenness. There are only trees and, between them, a rare river. There are no villages, only tree houses, and they are as rare as the rivers. The sky is now vast, primordial, filled with a terrifying silver light.

And yet after only an hour we were circling the abandoned missionary station; the house could be seen to one side of the strip, its roof covered with creepers and epiphytes. For some days I had felt increasingly unreal—an unreal man in an unreal place—and nothing could shake me out of this feeling. It had become a very real intuition. Those huts, that path, the swarming forest—it was not a part of my psyche.

From the air, Wanggemalo appeared as an oblong hole in the canopy, at the bottom of which lay a grass runway as long as a suburban lawn. There were a few huts instead of tree houses, and a path ran between them. To land here was like simply dropping vertically out of the air like a stone. The pilot made a face. He would keep the engine running as we disembarked.

In the forest, the drone of an airplane is a phenomenal event. It can be heard for half an hour before the plane itself arrives, and so the entire population of Wanggemalo—about the size of two rugby teams—had turned out at the end of the runway to greet us. They were a harrowing sight. Dressed in hand-me-down rags, they waited patiently for us, holding arrows, tethered flying foxes, and bundles of yellow flowers, their hair fluffed with chicken feathers, their legs spattered with toffee-colored mud. These were the "city" Kombai, if you will, the Wanggemalo clan, and in the hope of handouts they agreed to keep the airstrip grass trimmed so that planes could land. As we struggled up to the abandoned house, they followed without pestering us, fingering elegant arrows whitened at the tips and barbed like Gothic spires. Spontaneously, the boys carried the heavier bags.

Suddenly we were in heat again. The forest sang with ear-splitting cicadas. It was a sound unlike anything—unlike the russet cicadas of the American forest, unlike the sibilant creatures of the Andaman forests. This was a wall of sound made up of a dozen different pitches. I recognized at once the haunting, shrill sound of the cicadas that inhabit Japanese movies and that Japanese filmmakers have always used with such skill in creating sinister summer scenes. It sounds almost like a child crying. After a few minutes, this animal cacophony began to subdue something in my own mind; I gritted my teeth.

The Kombai did not sweat in the heat, though butterflies and sweat flies swirled around their heads, and they flowed silently in and out from among the hardwood trees that stood around us like towering scaffolds. Or else like ruined apartment blocks. For the jungle is indeed a beautiful nightmare that makes me think of a destroyed city, Berlin 1945, perhaps, or a giant cemetery. It is not for our delectation, boys and girls. Tufts of flowering ginger baked in the sun. Ailanthus trees rubbed together in a hot wind like giant reeds.

In the house, calendars frozen in the year 1994 still decorated the walls, along with children's drawings illustrating the story of Noah's Ark in Dutch. Outside, an abandoned baptismal font lay under the trees like a rotting swimming pool. It was as if the Lord and the jungle had struggled for dominion and the Lord had lost his footing. A piano still stood in the front room; a boy in parrot feathers sat in front of it, hammering a single out-of-tune key. But there was also a large verandah with decayed rattan chairs. In the children's room, Juha and I could share a bunk bed colonized by small red spiders.

The Kombai gathered in front of the verandah, arms filled with lizard-skin pipes and their sugarcane arrows. Women to one side, their hair shorn short with bamboo knives, men to the other. The latter stood hand in hand, dressed only in white *kotekas* made of hornbill beaks or halved acorn nuts, imposing bows slung across their backs. We stared at each other in silence, the whites' skin crawling with flies; they frowned with a child's intensity and watched our cigarettes and lighters carefully. For an hour no one much stirred. A drop of sweat fell into my eye. At the tops of the trees unknown birds came into focus, then dropped out again, as if departing from the present dimension.

The men then loosened up a bit and came up to shake our hands. They murmured *"Nari, nari,"* Kombai for "father." Their teeth were red from betel, the gums corroded; their skin bubbled with ringworm. There was a shy, fluttering quality to them, a nervous birdlike hopping and darting. The handshake was so limp that it was more like a mere brushing of the palms. No masculinity to be proved; the huge arrows were ubiquitous. They grinned, then stopped grinning, then grinned again. Our own grinning was the same. We stepped forward one by one and did the hand brushing. Soon, the women latched onto Theresia with cries of *"Nani, nani,"* or "mother." It was a pattern of sexual division we would see again and again, the world divided into two halves. In their bushy sago fiber skirts, the women were wary of the strange males; they watched us for a long time before venturing a quick handshake. After some hours of this exhausting negotiation, the sun began to drop. At first it dropped imperceptibly, as always, but around four it plummeted rapidly into the tree line. Dusk on the equator lasts about ten minutes. Ominous clouds began to mass, prickly with electricity.

A toothless midget appeared in a shredded bomber jacket. He strode up with a posse of young men as prospective porters, crowding onto the verandah in plastic flip-flops and galoshes, laying down their bows first. His arms were thin and strong as metal rods. Wanggemalo's chief, Brimob, is a legend among the Kombai—he gained his name by shooting the Indonesian captain of a Brimob mobile militia unit through the eye with an arrow. Papua's war of secession from Indonesia simmers always in the background, though is rarely discussed with foreigners. Occasionally, the Indonesians get the worst of it. The chief was all cackles and gags, horseplay, and fast-changing moods.

Brimob: "If you fuck our women, we'll cut your head off."

We all laughed. Brimob rocked back on his heels.

"No, actually"—he laughed along—"we *will* cut your head off."

The sun sank into the ironwoods, blazing its last flames. The horizon became one of gaunt arboreal silhouettes.

Juha turned quietly to me. "He says he'll cut our heads off. Fortunately, I would have to say that the girls are not a temptation."

"What if they were a temptation?"

They stared back, potbellied, their legs looking somehow frail beneath the formless sago skirts.

Darkness shot outward from the forest. It was like a hand swallowing up the house.

An oil lamp was lit. Brimob and Kelly picked out our porters, and I noticed that many of them had missionary names: a small boy called Nehemiah, another called Josiah. My own porter-to-be was Stephanus. There was even, alas, a Judas. They had seen white people before and they knew how to horse around with us. Nehemiah began to follow me around and pull faces, so I showed him some boogie-woogie moves and decided to call him Boogie-Woogie Baby. He must have been about six, but the Kombai never know how old they are.

There was no doubt a subtle colonial whiff about us as we sat in our cane chairs surveying the scene, though this time the gin and tonics would not be forthcoming. In the flare of the oil lamp, a circle of mute faces watched us— Wanggemalo's only entertainment.

I asked Georg what he was feeling.

"I don't know," he said. "The great weirdness of this. I have been to jungles before. The Amazon, Borneo—but not like this. Nothing like this."

"And who is that?" It was Theresia's voice and her finger pointed at two shadows sauntering across the airstrip. They were visible only when a flash of lightning erupted.

It was only now we realized that Brimob had departed and only a few Kombai were left lounging on the porch on their sides, elegantly smoking their pipes. A raffish adolescent sauntered onto the verandah, followed by a barefoot companion in a shaggy green jacket, on one arm of which could be read the word LINMAS. The latter was the village policeman—if that is the right word—shadowing an "arrested person" in a forest form of house arrest. They sat down gaily enough and took the pipe being passed around. The man in the LINMAS jacket was talkative and suave. He talked excitedly, thrusting his hands left and right as if indicating things unseen far off in the forest. The boy, he said, was a suspected witch. A *suangi.*

Suangi is the Indonesian term for a witch. The Kombai are obsessed with witches, for which their own term is *kakua-kumu. Kakua-kumu* are thought to be demons living in the forest who can assume human form, but equally those of a mouse, a cuscus, or a bird. The dying often name a *kakua-kumu* as responsible for their illness. The Kombai then form a hunting party and track down the witch to kill him. The *kakua-kumu* is cut into four parts; his brains and viscera are cooked on hot stones and eaten, after which the four parts are buried in the corners of the clan's territory. There was one thing that we had to avoid being called in the forest: a *kakua-kumu*. It was almost as bad as being an Indonesian.

"Oh, the Indonesians," the men said. "We just kill them as soon as they get off the plane."

The boy bared his teeth and a demented titter came out of him. They began to eat some cooked bat and, looking up a little fearfully, I noted the instantaneous disappearance of the last patch of lit blueness.

A witch among the Kombai is tried in ways that medieval Europeans would have found familiar. It is essentially a trial by ordeal. The suspect is made to eat vile things: frogs, pig shit, or even the human variety. His vomiting pattern will decide his fate. Omens and signs are taken into consideration. As for us, the Kombai might not always know we were entirely human, for we certainly didn't look human to them. It was best to wash as little as possible, even avoiding shampoo and shaving products for a while, for the forest people sometimes think that shampoo smells *suangi*-like. The less chemical we smelled, the more normal we would seem, the more human. The Kombai were known to get unpredictably aggressive when they smelled shampoo. Woolford winked at me and then at the *kakua-kumu*. The latter laughed again, baring betel-red gums. His eyes were indeed slightly insane. "*Nari,*" he said.

"Do you think he really is a witch?" Juha asked urbanely.

The "policeman" looked up, and smoke drifted out of his nostrils.

"*Kakua.*" The voice was a tense murmur.

Our sorcerer cheerfully asked for another cigarette. A ripple of anxiety touched the others as he walked among them. He and his warden stayed for an hour, then, presumably bored, sauntered off again across the airstrip.

The other boys got up and yawned. There is no electricity in Wanggemalo, and its people are too poor to own candles, let alone flashlights—they cannot get batteries, anyway. When the lightning flashed—as it did mutely, with no thunder—we saw the Kombai still standing there watching us. Our skins dripped. Woolford reached up and turned off the oil lamp.

"If there's a light they'll stay all night. Leave your flashlights off and they'll go away."

But an old woman remained on the verandah until nine, her nose bristling with cassowary quills, holding a live bat on a tether. From time to time, her eyes lowered, she asked us if we would like to buy it for dinner. Receiving no reply, she nonchalantly cut off its head and sat there with it in the burned grass, until fat warm raindrops came down and made her rise.

The missionaries would have called this monsoon "biblical." On the bunk bed, I was unable to sleep. Water crashed down from the rickety eaves of the porch on the far side of the glassless windows and formed black pools in the grass. The lightning was pink, then green—the green of a cheap candy. Juha snored. I got up in my socks and wandered out to feel the cool of the storm, a break in the unbearable heat. The runway seemed to have turned into a lake. The rain collected in three or four buckets laid around the house; I stepped out to catch the water and cool down. It was only when I was here that I remembered that I had been dreaming about the agonizing death of my grandfather. I stepped back onto the porch and saw at once that an old man was sitting cross-legged in a corner on some palm fronds, his face lit by the glow of a lizard-skin pipe.

"*Pagi*," I said, trying Indonesian. Good morning.

"*Umbiago.*"

By the side of the house, Penus was battling in the downpour to build a large cooking fire under a piece of bark. Kombai stood about in the mist, holding banana leaves above their heads. I sat in one of the rattan chairs and ate a box of my own Fig Newtons. It was the only one I had brought with me and now it was gone. Penus came up with a cup of hot chocolate, made from an Indonesian powdered mix called Milo, of which we had about four thousand sachets.

"You up four o'clock. Now we leave one hour. Get dressed!"

"Will the rain stop?"

"Always stop." The Jolly Green Giant guffaw. "Look-a mud."

"Can we walk in that?"

Penus scratched his beautiful head. One could not say. As if mud was a fickle spirit.

Porters now began to appear on the porch, kicking off soaked Wellies. They were very good-humored. *Pagi! Umbiago! Nari!* This time they had fewer bows, and balls of sago palm fiber flour wrapped in leaves. Traveling food. Was it the rain that put them in so good a mood? Or the thought of weeks of free food and a wage? There was a powwow at five and Woolford discussed the trail with a guide who had appeared out of the early morning: a tiny, slippery man called Yanbu. Yanbu knew all the most desolate, remote tree houses. A little over five feet, old by Kombai standards though probably not past forty, Yanbu wore a pair of Arsenal shorts, a dapper dog-tooth necklace, and a pair of rubber galoshes: jungle chic. A palm fiber *noken* bag hung from his forehead and he carried a large wok above it like a helmet. Impossible not to think of a crazy black Don Quixote searching not for windmills but for brides—because Yanbu was on the hunt for a paramour. A previous candidate had died, and he had relatives dispersed throughout the forest. He passed his pipe around and somehow the smoke dried out the spirit after all the rain. He stroked our arms and muttered things in Kombai. He had the frame of a fourteen-year-old boy; he spoke some crude Bahasa Indonesian and Kombai and flipped between them in every sentence—the indispensable jungle interpreter. Fortunately, Bahasa is an easy language for a European to learn, being neither tonal nor grammatically complex. Kombai, by contrast, is a trial. Apart from its complexity, it is all but impossible to find a written grammar or lexicon for it. Yanbu walked out into the mud and held out a hand. The rain was not as strong. We had to leave now, anyway, because it would take eight hours to reach the first tree house and the Kombai will not bivouac in the open forest for fear of *kakua-kumu*. We drank some Milo and ate some bright purple fried taro, heavily salted. The rain would not stop all day.

As the sky lightened and the trees became green again, hazed behind heavy mists, we struck out through the wet huts toward the sago swamps. The twenty-five porters formed a column a quarter mile long, bristling with weapons, woks, biscuit tins, and tent bags. The boys sang and twanged bamboo harps. Boogie-Woogie Baby did the boogie-woogie. In the doors of the shacks, the women sat with their children, staring but not waving, and soon we were on the other side, in the dripping rattan glades that seemed to guard the entrance to the forest.

Wanggemalo is surrounded by dense sago palm swamps, miles of thick slime that have to be crossed over a network of fallen logs. Soaked in a toxic mix of sweat, deet repellent, and black mud smelling of fermenting beer—the rotting sago palms—we struggled through them like high-wire artists without poles. It was a point of anticolonial pride for me to carry my own pack; why else had I labored on the beach in Seminyak for so many weeks? The boys protested, but I faced them down. Heaving the pack onto both shoulders, I mounted the first log, which rolled under pressure, and made the dare. Halfway across I felt my legs giving out. The log rolled again, and I crashed into the swamp. Stephanus whipped away the pack as I fell and nimbly spirited it across to the next log. I climbed back on and had to lie for a while getting my breath back.

Lashed by the rain, I lay there like a stricken pig, watching the boys laughing, though not cruelly. I wondered if I could do this. If I gave up here, however, I would have to spend a month in Wanggemalo, probably eating flying foxes in exchange for a wristwatch. I was not fat, but I was too fat. I would have to lose ten pounds quickly, to acquire the Kombai body, which is built for speed and the avoidance of error. Even without the pack, I was the slowest, the most buffoonish, and Yanbu stopped frequently to let me catch up, a delicate look of pity on his face. What manner of man was this that could not walk on slippery logs? Who could not race up sudden inclines laced with gigantic armor-piercing thorns? He did not approve of shoes or clothes, since they were clearly a hindrance of the highest order. I often wondered what Yanbu thought of us. His face was mostly amused, perplexed, on the border of some kind of disbelief.

Yanbu was an indispensable ambassador, for there is a protocol for visiting tree houses, a delicate diplomacy whose rules must be followed to the letter. Emissaries would be sent to the tree house the day before, offering gifts—usually tobacco—and asking permission to enter the premises. The Kombai love to smoke, though usually they use raw leaves; in remoter tree houses, tobacco is at first unfamiliar but quickly acquires a certain prestige. If the men in the tree houses like the tobacco and permission is granted, Yanbu will then approach the place and try to calm the excited occupants. There would usually be a brief display of ritual force, a standoff that might express complex anxieties: strangers roaming where they do not belong, religious sacrilege, or even the belief that we might be sorcerers. Throughout our trek, in fact, Yanbu was a key figure, and an enigmatic one. Was he uncomfortable between the two worlds? When I looked at my photographs later, I noticed that Yanbu was the only Kombai who looked into the camera. A smile always bent the mouth, but downward.

The swamp was cleared in three hours. We collapsed among some rotting sago set in a series of swamp pools and reapplied the deet. Encephalitic malaria roams the Papua forest. The boys loafed and it was clear they were only slightly winded. The little ones went off to hunt for lizards, and we mastered our first Kombai and Bahasa words, exchanging them with the porters while smoking. Their average age was probably about eighteen. They began to yell our names. *Ju-ha. Lo-rry.* Bellicose foot stamping, warlike cries of *uey, uey!* The moroseness of Wanggemalo wore off, and suddenly this tangled submarine forest filled with arpeggios of laughter. We had to eat our first sago balls. It was like munching on pieces of damp house plaster, the starch sucking all the moisture out of the mouth and leaving it tastelessly dry.

The rain eased off. Farther on, the forest darkened; thorned vines swung down from on high. "Forests," Joseph Roth wrote, "are where a landscape hides its secrets." And here the secrecy was stifling. Near-invisible trails ran like silken threads from tree house to tree house, and along these lines the Kombai walked with an unconscious assurance, like sleepwalkers—as if they could have walked them with no eyes. As we went along them ourselves, I wondered merely what they meant and where they led. How many tree houses were thus connected and how many paths were also used by other peoples, like the fearsome Korowai next door? The paths ran along crests, down ravines, across swamps, across fields of primeval ferns taller than me, and glades of carellia trees. Delicate pitcher plants with crimson lids dotted the borders, their vases filled with dead flies. Very rarely, a cream-white orchid sprouted out of a tree in imitation of a road sign. Soon, earth's largest butterflies ventured out into the drier air, huge black creatures as large as small birds, like angels in medieval frescoes. Attracted perhaps by the heat, they settled on our heads.

My breathing was now so strained that I had to slow my body against its will. During rests, I felt my pulse hammer inside the temples. I became addicted to Yanbu's pipe because it was a calmant. If I smoked and counted to two hundred, my heart rate came down to a peaceable level and I could breathe again. With his bevy of instruments, Georg was able to tell us a few things: that it was 101 degrees in the shade, that the humidity level was 94 percent, and that on the GPS map the area we were in was marked "no data." And there were very few places in the world that were marked "no data." Thus, in the viewfinder of our omniscient technology, our dubious paradise did not even exist. We were nowhere, anywhere—wherever we happened to be. The Kombai didn't have a name for this forest. It was The Forest, and there was nothing outside it.

By three in the afternoon, the terrain had changed. We now slaved up the sides of mossy ravines slippery as glass, carpeted with leaves, then slid down them toward stagnant streams: an obstacle course carved out of salmon-pink mud, trip-wire vines, and hidden snakes. Impotent rage began to well up in me, for in nature the "developed" man quickly becomes a helpless child, dependent upon people whom we have been conditioned to think of as helpless children. The inversion of roles is not flattering. Indifferent to our sufferings, however, the porters chanted Kombai songs, and I could hear them far ahead, keeping rhythm with each other like rowers as they slipped through the forest. Their easy relentlessness spelled dementia for the rest of us. I was soon at the far rear of the column with Penus, who kept me alive with jokes and kept my soaring pessimism at bay.

At the end of the afternoon, however, we began to slow. The forest thinned a little; tall spindle-thin palms emerged into a visible sky. Yanbu yodeled into the forest ahead. We were at the edge of the first tree house. Like echoes of Yanbu's voice, the same cries came back. Understanding the moment, everyone fell quiet and the cries drifted back and forth, a jungle opera sung in falsetto.

Woolford had taken an English investment banker along this same trail the year before. This tree house, therefore, would not be a pure first contact. It didn't matter. The scene was surreal enough. We were on the edge of a sun-flooded clearing piled with the debris of hundreds of shattered trees. It looked like the site of a meteor strike, without the crater.

But from its center rose a gabled thatch house on sixty-foot stilts, a wondrous sight, like a smaller Ark stranded in the treetops by the Flood. Its bamboo walls were covered with shields painted white and ocher red. It swayed in the wind, smoke puffing out of its door. A naked man stood below it, his bow drawn, his hornbill *koteka* quivering. He looked mildly homicidal.

To one side stood a long house of sago thatch, the ceiling festooned with mouse skulls. The naked one came creeping toward us, his bow suddenly drawn tighter, his face contracted with a kind of haggard anxiety. The sugarcane arrow was a yard long and delicately barbed, finely carved with mouse teeth and painted with white bands. In one dexterous bow hand he held a kind of sandwich made of sago stuffed with fat white capricorn beetle grubs from the sago's interior. A "sago burger" we would later call it. Ever ready for an anthrotourist frisson, Georg volunteered to carry the plastic bag of Indonesian tobacco.

From a distance, we noticed that the naked one was shaking. Georg reached out to touch his hand. The Kombai extended his, shaking like an epileptic, then quickly withdrew it and violently shook his head. They tried again. The fourth time, their hands grazed and the tension subsided as quickly as it had arisen. The Kombai straightened up, loosened the arrow, and poked into the bag of tobacco. Quite unexpectedly, he smiled with a line of rotten teeth. *"Nari,"* he said.

We stepped forward, half whispering *nari, nari, nari* and passing our hands over his. Our antagonist turned charmingly friendly. He pointed at our penises with a little smirk and said, *"Ringi bangus?"* This caused a moment's confusion but was swiftly translated: "Shall we wrap your dicks?"

We inquired into the specifics of this operation. It involved folding back the foreskin of the peccant member and pushing the whole organ inside the body. The first time you did it, apparently, you passed out with nausea, but it would certainly get you "in" with the Kombai. Only after the reinsertion could you get the apparatus to be small enough to be wrapped. The results were elegant, no doubt, but after a ten-second conference we decided to refuse. The man tutted and shook his head. That was not the spirit. And he had offered to do it for us.

"All right." He sighed, eyeing the tobacco bags. "Come in anyway."

Behind the tree house, a trail dropped across a stream to a long house buried in the jungle. A dark tea-colored river curled past it. Here the porters pitched camp—tents for us, the house for them. In seconds, they assembled a crude table with benches fashioned out of branches and bamboo twine, a miracle of forest engineering that they repeated every night. To one side, we saw the house low on the ground where the women slept (only men sleep in the tree houses). Still rattled, Georg, Juha, and I swam naked in the cold little river, and the extreme whiteness of our bodies looked surpassingly strange in that dark water. White ghosts. The Kombai later confessed that they didn't want to touch us because they thought we might be incredibly cold. I wondered, though, how Georg had felt handing over the tobacco to our first forest Kombai. Had he been suitably unnerved by this planned brush with the exotic?

"I could see the whole thing was ceremonial. But that look in his eye—it was incredible. I've never seen a look like that. I don't even know what emotion it was."

What did he think it was?

"At first I thought terror. But it was more complex than that."

What is more complex than terror? I thought.

"Paralysis?"

"I don't know. I don't know what to think."

"But he's seen a white man before," Juha said.

It seemed such a quaint phrase: *seen a white man before.*

"Did you see his knees shake?" I said.

"I wonder if he would have killed me if I'd done something unexpected."

Georg shook his head and fell silent. His beard was now

darkening his face and, like all of us, his hair was getting a little wild and Robinson Crusoe–like. Brilliant lemon butterflies sat absurdly on his head. Of all of us, he had the most persistent, childlike curiosity, which I suppose is the irresistible curiosity of all scientists. I wondered if his trip to Papua was the outgrowth of a sixties romanticism that Juha and I—being too young—didn't have. Or whether it was just the result of a relentless exploration of the planet that had reached its apogee here. Why, for that matter, do we pursue a relentless exploration of the planet when the thing that most interests us ultimately is ourselves? Where would he and Theresia go from here?

"It's a good question," he admitted moodily. "Underwater, perhaps."

At dusk, we set up candles on the table and waited for the onslaught of the evening mosquitoes. "Encephalitic malaria," Georg began to say, raising a scientific finger. But we knew all about encephalitic malaria.

Feral yells echoed through the forest. Without warning, two phantom figures suddenly emerged from the trees, daintily chiseled bodies adorned with white hornbill *kotekas* and bird of paradise feathers woven into their hair, mouse tails tied around their heads. Saying not a word, they glided aloofly past us, lighting their way with a sheaf of burning grass. They shot wide-eyed looks at us, but principally at the hard, lucid flames of the candles. When they shook our hands, I saw the white ringworm coating their shoulders. I thought they sniffed us a little, to see what our smell was: human or other.

During the night I woke in my tent. The porters' fire stabbed against the trees and the night was filled with the laughter of small children. Boogie-Woogie Baby and Josiah playing tag. The harps twanging monotonously. It was remarkable how much laughter filled the Kombai nights. Somewhere nearby a man was singing, a rippling rolling of vowels and tones that must have been thousands of years old, proof—if we are in Rousseau mode—of the claim that human speech might have originated with birds. The Kombai seemed never to sleep and their sounds never relented: laughter that runs on and on without shape, songs that never stop and that drive you mad.

For centuries, primitive cultures have been at the heart of both utopian thought and tourism—at least since Montaigne wrote "On Cannibals" and Rousseau his 1755 *Discourse on the Origin of Inequality*. "Nothing is more gentle," Rousseau famously wrote, "than man in his primitive state." After Cook and Bougainville first visited the South Sea Islands in the mid-eighteenth century, Enlightenment philosophes thought that the truth of human nature could now finally be revealed by an empirical study of primitive societies. In his *Supplément au voyage de Bougainville*, tardily published in 1796, Diderot eloquently made the case that primitive cultures like Tahiti were joyful because they were sexually free, unburdened by neurotic artifice. Tahitians, he argued, were noble because they allowed themselves to be changeable, just as Nature is. And so it was into this mythology, surely, that Mead came as a young woman, however bright and novel her journey to the South Seas must have seemed. An expectation had probably been raised inside the unconscious. And the culmination of that journey, for her, was Papua.

I was careful to bring her *Letters* with me, because there

is no substitute for reading the most renowned work on Papua while being actually there. Mead had not worked in this region—most of her Papuan fieldwork was done on the Sepik River in the north, a river that straddled both PNG and Irian Jaya. No two Papuan peoples are the same, and though I didn't know the Sepik, I could tell from her descriptions that it was a very different topography and landscape. It was impossible to imagine a wide-open riverscape white with elephant grass inside a suffocating jungle like this. Mead is a great travel writer because she is not a travel writer. Her images stay in the mind: the tiny babies painted with pink clay like roses against their mothers' dark skin; the children similarly daubed, their faces red and their bodies yellow; the shaman's dance among dead crocodiles after a hunt; the mud heads sculpted by the village children along the banks of the river. During night feast, "men of importance standing up and ordering the moon to come out, so that there would be no rain." The land is rendered with small, accurate strokes:

> To turn suddenly from the quite unbelievable proportions of the Sepik into a narrow stream which flows between high banks, on which thinly leafed trees are set like worn-out sketches against the sky, where the lotus leaves are green when they lie flat and pink when the wind catches them, ruffling them up off the water which itself has a changeable pink and green powder on its darkness—this is to find oneself in a land to which one might conceivably belong.

I could not feel anything like this about the rain forest because there was no openness, no expanses of water here. But the people were like bolts of pure nervous energy in this stifling context, and they could not but remind me of the Iatmul among whom Mead lived on the Sepik in 1938, in the village of Tambunam:

> These Iatmul are a gay, irresponsible, vigorous people, always either laughing or screaming with rage. The two types of behavior are more or less alternating and seem to give them about equal satisfaction. Children learn to yell for every satisfaction, and later they decide it was the yelling they enjoyed. When anyone loses his or her temper, the bystanders stand about, grinning from ear to ear, feeling reassured that this is a world in which people can lose their tempers HARD . . . For they are not cruel or stingy or greedy. They have no infanticide, they look after their poor and orphaned, they share their food and betel and tobacco with a lavishness which their food supply hardly justifies and they lose their tempers all over the place, without guilt or shame.

During the long journey from Dubai to the Kombai, I had found myself slowly falling in love with the young Margaret Mead of the 1930s. Perhaps it was the effect of having her constantly there at night, by candlelight, and now when I was alone in my tent rested on an unrolled length of tree bark that served as a replacement for a damaged and useless Therm-a-Rest mattress. I read with a headlamp, with the shapes of orb-weaver spiders silhouetted on the netting, and the solitude was greater than anything one can conceive in the century of ubiquitous electric light, because the forest was so dark that nothing shone through it, and even the fire of the Kombai a few hundred yards away was just a dull orange reflection against their faces. A book—the murmur of writing itself—has an amorous intimacy here; it's an artifact hauled into the place where it doesn't belong. (The Kombai found books baffling. Were they stores of tobacco sheets for smoking?) But a book by a woman is not the same as one written by a man; I asked myself if I could "fall in love" with a female writer. It was not quite possible. It had never happened before, except, if I am to come clean, with the New Zealand writer Keri Hulme, a writer I love and whom my peers so often affect to despise. It cannot be helped; few writers have a real voice, and when one does, the effect is nothing less than amorous. It is not that I especially admire women writers as a group or feel any need to express solidarity with them—that tedious bromide is irrelevant. It is just that Mead has a voice *in the act of travel*.

Nevertheless, I had to wonder if her picture of the Iatmul, like that of the Samoans—like my frivolous impression of the Kombai—was nothing more than a lyrical Diderotian mistake. If you happen upon a land in which you could conceivably belong, a fierce drive is unlocked from inside your tight, disciplined ego, a new passion: a yearning for belonging, I suppose. It is this that makes your responses to lands and peoples—and readers—amorous. But it doesn't necessarily make them accurate.

After a storm, during which tons of leaves were shaken down onto the tents, the morning cleared. A drenching heat poured from the white sky, the giant trees singing like telegraph poles.

Georg and Theresia took out their reference books and with them scanned the forest canopy with gingerly sensitive and academic vigor. They were admirable jungle companions—tough, stoic, and open to subtle moods. After hours of harsh bushwhacking, Theresia finally spotted a rare lizard, an emerald tree monitor, scuttling up a tree so far above us that the naked eye couldn't detect it. *"Schön!"* she exclaimed. "Where?" the porters shouted. "There!" from the innocent scientist. The porters rushed to surround the tree and began scampering up after it on liana straps.

Theresia turned to her lover. "A beauty!"

Georg looked through a book to see if he could find it listed. *Varinus prasinus prasinus?*

They followed the climbers' progress through the binoculars as they laughed their way up to the canopy. A few seconds later the lizard came tumbling down. "Oh dear," Theresia moaned, turning quite pale.

The boys jumped on the dazed reptile and gaily beat out its brain with sticks. Holding it up by its tail, they showed it off—a huge three-foot specimen with jewellike markings—while blood dripped off its tongue. Dinner, it appeared. Theresia picked up her walking stick and moved on, with a repressed indignation, I suspect, and even a twinge of rage. Cockatoos—those beautiful creatures—would prove an even more anguishing problem. The boys liked them roasted on spits. Birds of paradise? Excellent cooked on hot stones. What to the educated Westerner is a marvel of Nature to be cataloged in a digital camera is to the Kombai a wood-smoked snack.

This forest was dense: quick-stick thickets with gray-green bark, yemane trees, and wet leech limes. Gum trees soared up to its canopy, merging into eaglewoods—an exotic tree that in recent years has become a source of income to tribes in the interior of Papua. Known as *ud* in the Arab world, it yields the world's most valuable incense. In Singapore, it trades for hundreds of dollars an ounce. In Indonesia it is called *gaharu*. Like cocaine, it spawns a dark black-market trade. The Papuan rebels, known as the OPM, sometimes kill *gaharu* collectors in the remote forests, considering them traitors and profiteers. The Kombai were not collecting *gaharu* yet. But it was probably only a matter of time.

Shaggy pandanus glittered in little glades of ficus trees. Yanbu sliced through barbed vines and primeval ferns with a machete. We slithered along fallen trees, stopping in the rivers to drench ourselves and refill the bottles, shaking them up with iodine tablets. The word for crocodile, *boya*, hovered on the lips. Then there were stillnesses that lasted hours. The trees moving as if in a trance, the tops waving sadly. The loneliness of the world's deepest forest. You hear nothing but your own heart and then, out of nowhere, the rustling of water far away, sliding over fallen trees. A dreamlike fear. You think back to Hansel and Gretel, the forests of our past. It is a form of travel into the remote past, into our primitivity before we settled down to fields and houses, and time began. There is a barbarian core to us. One could say it is the core that is still alive, still sending out its pulses through the psyche. But it can be fully reawakened. For soon I could hear it inside my mind, a running voice full of violence and tempest, longing to hold a bow, keeping pace with the psychic electricity of the Kombai.

————

After seven hours, we reached the next tree house. It was lofty, with grand views over the forest, like a weightless Italian landscape painting; all misted blues and feathery horizons, but with a feeling of suffocating isolation. Juha went forward with the tobacco, the three men there yelling into his face and running around him with the arrows pointed at his chest. I think his blue eyes unnerved them deeply. But tobacco calms all things eventually, and there came a moment when we all sat down and the big lizard-hide pipes were lit and the men came up sheepishly and took our hands with a shy *"Nari, nari."*

That night, over *nasi goreng* (fried rice with whatever other ingredients are at hand) and brush turkey eggs, we asked two Kombai elders living there about their myths. The old men were gritty and stern; hideous bark earrings distorted their lobes. One was called Vedawayo and the other man was his son. They sat next to our single candle, which was fixed to the edge of the table amid a storm of moths. They stared at the candle. "It burns," they said, "but it doesn't go out." And they clicked a finger behind their front teeth, a gesture, like *koteka* wriggling, that translates as "Wow!" To turn them away from their wonderment to ours, we asked them about their beliefs.

The neighboring Korowai believe that the world is made of three concentric circles. At the center are the living; around them live the dead. And beyond both is a great body of water that they call The Great Dog, where the dead reside. The Kombai, however, were reluctant to divulge their cosmology, regarding it as a pious secret that should not be revealed to outsiders. They merely recounted their creation myth. Once upon a time, the human race lived like grubs inside a large *noken* bag high up in a tree house. They were fed sago until one day, having grown big, they spilled out and learned how to multiply, coming down from the primordial tree house to the earth.

As they told us this, they ate live sago grubs from a piece of bark, first breaking their necks, then biting into the fatty flesh. And what about *kakua-kumu*?

"Ah, sorcerers are everywhere!" Vedawayo said, shaking his head bitterly. "I killed one years ago. I ate him. But that was years ago. Not now."

They looked down between their knees at the ground, avoiding our eyes, though not, it seemed, out of shame. Their tone was matter-of-fact.

"Would you eat one now?"

Nods. There was no other way of annihilating them completely. "I killed one," the son said, "but I didn't eat him. I tied him up and shot him dead. I threw him into the river and then drank the water mixed with blood."

Because the soul for the Kombai resides in the brain and the stomach, it is these two items that have to be eaten if the evil spirit is to be destroyed efficiently. So we were surprised the son had not eaten the brains.

I then asked them where they thought we came from.

A dry, indecisive sigh. "We don't know. Some of us thought you might be from the forest where the sun rises, others said the forest where the sun sets. But we don't know which."

"We don't come from the forest," Woolford said.

When it was translated by Yanbu, they stared stonily at the ground. What did that mean? Woolford went on: "We come from outside the forest."

At this, they shook their heads direly and clucked. Outside the world? How was that possible?

Even Yanbu looked doubtful. Did we really come from where we said we did? What lay beyond The Forest if not The Great Dog?

Neither man had ever heard of Wanggemalo.

"What happens," Juha tried, "when you die?"

They shrugged and, for some reason, scratched their balls. "Your soul goes walking in the forest."

The conversation had a curiously veiled quality. The Kombai do not lightly divulge things about themselves to strangers. But there was also the problem of language, which none of us could solve. Yanbu and the Kombai often drifted off into discussions of their own, as if Yanbu was grappling with concepts impossible for him to translate into Bahasa. I remembered then the poor Tasaday of the Philippines, who had apparently gotten so sick of prying outsiders that when interviewed they fell into a fantastical private language called "nafnaf," in which all the words ended with the sound "naf" and that no professional linguist could understand.

Later, I fell into a severe exhaustion in my tent. For the first time since we had set out, I felt morbid and unhinged. I watched the outlines of praying mantises crawling over the mosquito nets, their bodies glistening and pulsating. A bright pink spider the size of my hand suddenly ran across it. The jungle's gorgeous horror: how beautiful were the giant funnel spiders that can kill a parrot. Beetles orange as coral, fiery ants strung out on hanging vines as they marched vertically toward the canopy. The insect world that is never still for a second, that cannot sleep.

More bubbling laughter now echoed through the trees and, for the first time, I felt a sullen contentment under which the unhinged hysteria still simmered—a change in the body, perhaps, as it adjusted to the ferocity of nature. My notebooks had already crumbled into clots of wet paper and I was relieved. Everything rots in the jungle, but of course this is desirable in the end. What remains is a deliciously moronic survival in the face of all the mantises and spiders. The ecstasy of *not dying*.

In the morning, however, we awoke to a nightmare breakfast that almost annulled this feeling: our hosts had brought a large plate piled high with tiny roasted legs, so small that we had to eat about thirty of them each. They were disgusting, like caramelized pork chops hacked from a midget Frankenpig. They surely weren't the jungle delicacies I had previously hoped to avoid, bandicoot bladders, for example, or Blyth's hornbill eyes. We sucked on them like schoolboys, unable to get satisfaction. But what were they?

Yanbu's eyes were those of a loony Mother Goose as he explained, picking them up and turning them over like edible gemstones, as if to show how rare and precious they were—and what an honor it was for us to digest them. "Mouse hinds!"

A changed mood now swept over us, for the next tree house was going to be a very different excursion. Rumor had it that a pig feast was planned for the following night, and that several families would be present. This meant that there would be thirty or so Kombai in attendance. They were gathered to smooth over a delicate matter: earlier in the year a *kakua-kumu* had been murdered from one of the tree houses and the clan needed to heal the rift among its members. Pigs would be slaughtered by way of atonement, but the intrusion of strangers had not been anticipated.

This place was called Kalamburu. There was a bend in the trail as it rose toward a high crest denuded of trees, burned to a sienna hue and the stumps of cut boles left jutting up like black fangs. The column stopped in a field of huge ferns, and cries of greeting shot back and forth. As it happened, it was my turn to offer the tobacco. We could tell that the Kombai were excited; the cries were a little hysterical. And I would have to go in alone with Yanbu.

As I walked forward alone into the clearing, the sound of my feet on burned twigs was loud as firecrackers; the sudden shouts of the men swarming around me, however, were far more muted. At that moment, I wondered if all this was an elaborate mise-en-scène arranged behind our backs like the "native scenes" in Yanimura. After all, I was not an anthropologist. I knew nothing about these people. Perhaps they would come rolling down from their tree houses armed with digital cameras, crying, "All right, you white bastards, say cheese!" This suspicion passed. There were two magnificent tree houses, far taller than the others; the men retreated to them, pawing the ground and glaring at this incredible white creature, strange as a unicorn, holding a bag of Indonesian shag and tottering forward on shredded hiking boots. There were about twenty of them, their bows drawn. I inched forward, for there was nothing else to do. An arrow suddenly flew over my head with a satisfying basso sound—a *whoosh* corresponding to a shot of adrenaline. Then another. The missile flew into the trees behind me, where far behind me the porters hit the deck. Yanbu pulled a face forcibly stuck halfway between amusement and sardonic disdain. He said something jovial in Kombai, which must have been something like, "Don't worry, city boy, they don't miss!" A Kombai who means business will shoot you through the pupil at a hundred yards without blinking. But I felt like laughing as part of the same hysteria I had felt earlier in the day. It was a crowd of "natives" from a Bob Hope movie. The kinky warriors from Bali Hai!

An older man in a large hornbill *koteka* crept forward, a look of catatonic stupefaction on his face. He swayed from side to side, glassy-eyed. Quite suddenly, he pushed the arrow loaded in his bow forward and indicated that I should spear the tobacco packet on it. He didn't want to risk touching me. Slipping the tobacco off his arrow, he felt the alien plastic and licked it. An alien taste. He opened it and sniffed. An alien scent.

The meeting was bizarre for both of us, but there was a far-reaching imbalance in our respective preparations. He could not be prepared for my hair, my skin, my eyes, the texture of my industrial clothes, my watch and shoelaces, the musty smell of deet insect repellent, the copious sweat. It was not surprising that he could not bring himself to graze my hand, though he tried over and over, shaking his head, completely perplexed. I loomed over all of them, a great white Gulliver gone astray.

But by now Yanbu was there and urging him in Kombai to shake hands. His name was Chief Mamandeo. "*Nari, nari,*" I tried. And we began saying "*nari*" to each other, over and over, as if reassuring each other that we were both human after all. An hour later, they had all calmed down and were smoking our tobacco in their pipes large as didgeridoos, pulling expressions of snobbish disgust but smoking it all the same. "When we saw you," Mamandeo admitted, "we thought, *what could that be?* Then we were mad. Then we were scared shitless." They laughed. "We didn't kill you, though."

The pig feast lasted until dark. Frenzied dancing and songs as the forest dipped into a flame-thrower sunset, the men and women disappearing together in the jungle, leaving the white men alone on the ridge, gazing into mists and palms. The ocher and white shields on the sides of the tree houses caught the sun as it died, and the designs seemed clearly reminiscent of Australia's Aboriginal equivalents. Then the people returned as a tightly bonded mass, shouting together, fused into a collective trance. Our porters had joined them, mouse tails tied around their heads. When their eyes caught ours they held back the grins—the constipation induced by a very subtle betrayal.

The pig was cooked in stones wrapped in leaves, the hair scraped off with bamboo knives. As they ate apart from the women, the men scooped up blood in large oyster shells. We were offered the capricorn beetle grubs from the inside of the sago palms—huge, white beasts that are the Kombai equivalent of caviar. Crunching them alive, as the true Kombai gourmet must, was like biting into a sausage skin filled with explosive pus. When Mamandeo came down to the tents afterward to smoke with us, accompanied by two brothers, I wanted to know how they had acquired these shells. He shrugged. Trade with neighbors. So this was an example of vicarious contact that anthropologists liked to cite when proving to you that there is no such thing as an "uncontacted" people. But did he know they came from the sea?

"What is it, sea?"

We explained what sea was. Water, big, horizons. I tried to describe a whale. "Like a giant pig?" they asked. After that, I made a clumsy attempt to explain that I had flown here from Bali, which was not too far from Papua. They were both part of Indonesia.

"What is it, Indonesia?"

"A big country with many islands."

"Country?" The brows knitted.

The two brothers, Morgana and Andono, also discussed the matter between themselves. Finally they asked, "What is Papua?" Which brought the topic to an end.

Behind them, the brooding shapes of trees, a dark ruin. And the darkness here was gripping, filled with tension, so deep that nothing could stab through it except the energy of twentieth-century gadgets. As we sat at our crude table with the candles, men and boys swarmed round to stare at the bright images in our digital camera displays. The older men could not grasp what they were—they expressed fear of looking into the LCD—but the children were quick to grasp the idea of a difference in scale between image and reality.

Kelly asked them if they had seen a white man before.

Morgana: "We thought you might be people. But white skin? Ah, then we were shocked."

"Shocked?"

They shook their heads and spat.

"Shocked. Who knew men could be white? And women, too."

They groaned softly for a while, as if this was truly an appalling idea, as no doubt it is.

We said then that we had walked three hundred days to reach them (the equivalent of a plane journey from Europe, we thought), and this made them click their teeth and mutter, *"Haren!"* How about that?

Then there was the assorted campers' junk on the table. A tin of Gong Kuang Chinese biscuits from Jakarta, decorated with a sinister picture of a perfect American family sitting down to dinner—except that their eyes were subtly Chinese. *Suangis?* The plastic Nalgene water bottle with its ice-blue tint. The Kombai had never seen an artificial blue before, and this radical color struck them as extremely *haren.* As for cups and forks, they were incomprehensible. Our clothes were equally astonishing, and as always the candles were a sensation.

"We live in darkness," Andono said. "Could you bring us a candle if you come again?" Since his Kombai didn't have a word for candle, he used the Bahasa word we had used, *lilin.*

I then offered them our malted biscuits. With extreme caution they held them up to the candle, turned them over, inspected them gravely, then stuck out their tongues to graze the surface. They were nonplussed and deeply suspicious. Then, egged on by Yanbu, they bit tiny morsels off.

The Kombai have an elegant way of spitting. They form a blob of saliva on their lips, lean over, and let it fall silently.

Mamandeo: "It makes me want to vomit."

Next, a spoonful of white sugar. They nibbled at it and

then, with ineffable disgust, went through the same spitting motion.

Morgana: "It makes us want to vomit."

We tried a simple cup of water next. But it was the plastic that upset them, the feel of it against their lips. They spat it out.

Andono: "It makes me want to vomit."

Afterward, we walked back up to the crest, smoking with the men, while they lit their way with bunches of burning grass. Far across the forest, hundreds of fireflies blazed under flashes of lightning; points of burning grass swung to and fro below as people wound their way back to other tree houses. We listened for a long time to the Kombai men singing, the monotonous twanging of the bamboo harps. It was striking that men who ate witches could sing so gently. Some claimed never to have heard of their neighbors, the Korowai, and several had never heard of Wanggemalo. For a moment, I looked up and saw the Kombai men gathered around the last dying candle. The concept of wax had them mightily perplexed. So many boggled minds in so small a place! But it was surely a case of crossed wires, of endless misunderstandings. Our notion of change is integral to us; if Papuans have been on this island for thirty thousand years, then we are forced to marvel at both their ingenious adaptations and also, less piously, at their slow pace of change. We, congenital tourists, wondered why they didn't travel far and wide; they wondered why we did.

"But then," Juha pointed out, "why should they travel far and wide? They think *we're* mad for traveling far and wide. They must look at all our gear, our things, and think we're insane."

"We are insane," I said.

But there were the Kombai of and for themselves, charming and lusty. I liked them. They were hospitable and, when all was said and done, kind. They had humor—as much as anyone. More than the French, probably. And it was true that, talking about their "stasis," we were assuming that they were in some way outside of history. Yet hadn't Brimob only a few miles from here shot an Indonesian officer through the eye with an arrow? History surged around and through these "virgin" forests, an invisible poison. Hidden to the court of world opinion, the OPM waged its desperate guerrilla war of independence against the Islamic superstate. OPM units fought Brimob units with forgotten savagery. And then there was us.

I was woken at four a.m. by rain falling through my tent roof. It's a golden rule of camping to peg your rain fly before sleep, but this happy camper had failed to do so. Within seconds I was outside, naked, with a lamp on my head, struggling with the rain fly as a monsoon rain crashed down. Seconds more and I had become Laocoön and the Tent, a writhing mass of flesh and nylon, screaming abuse at pegs, ropes, and even my own hands. But there are moments that define the experience of a place, and as I was struggling with the intractable fly, soaked from head to foot and alone in the middle of the forest, I began laughing hysterically to myself, at myself. Looking up, I saw the Kombai warriors huddled together under one of the tree houses, patiently watching the scene. One can only imagine their thoughts confronted with this vision of white sanity and initiative. "Thirty thousand years, and they still can't figure out a rain fly."

At first light, a line of small boys passed by, returning

from the river in the mist, each one wearing a fresh white cockatoo feather in his hair and holding a tall tube of cane filled with water. They looked over at me with a sort of sorrow, the pity that the naked feel for the clothed.

A day's walk away, the next tree house was called Mamlumburu. The hike was brutal enough, but on the way we passed through a broad river of stunning cold water and stones as large and white as dinosaur eggs. Everyone stripped and began swimming—a fête champêtre! The water was colored like Lucozade, a British beverage of ages past, an acidic orange with green tints. The thirty-foot crocodiles for which Papua is renowned probably did not swim as far upriver as this, but we sent the boys ahead to watch for *boya*. Who has not seen the famous footage of African crocs nonchalantly tossing five-hundred-pound zebras and wildebeests into rivers by their snouts and tearing them to shreds? There were pools in which grown men could float, their whiteness open to the amazement of Boogie-Woogie and Joshua. For the little boys now followed me everywhere, hips a-go-go, crying "Boogie!" Cultural contamination flowing freely into innocent young minds.

At Mamlumburu, a young man named Gagerigo came out to meet us. He scowled as he chewed on a twig, and it took some time to persuade him and his old uncle, Mangualo, that we were not there to maliciously enchant them. Gagerigo wore a leaf and nothing else, and his look was somberly averted. Finally convinced, they took us up into the house, which swayed in a stormy wind. The floors were made of bamboo strips lashed together, and the walls were built around an actual tree. Inside, the sago ceilings were covered with mouse and fish heads blackened by the two fires that burned constantly. We lay there shattered after the walk and Gagerigo told us that he was more afraid of us than he was of cassowaries. He too had never seen a white before—none of them had—and as we lay panting with fatigue and watching the lightning over the canopy, they watched us warily, unblinking, but smoking our tobacco. Looking up, I saw that the ceiling was black not with soot but with the bodies of hundreds of small cockroaches.

During the evening, Mangualo told us that he didn't want to go to Wanggemalo because he was "scared of clothes." He then added that he would much prefer it if we were all naked like them.

"We would be less afraid if you were naked."

"We'll die of malaria," Juha said.

Mangualo plucked his pant material. "Why do you wear this shit?"

The Kombai rarely wash in rivers, in which we were always plunging at any opportunity. "It would be even better if you wore a *koteka* like us." I felt that he was on the brink of adding, "And you'd look a damn sight better, too!" For we were now five hobos in tattered clothes, filthy and lacerated with tiny cuts. It was just that the penile inversion operation made me think of Dr. Preecha.

"So, what do you say?" from Mangualo.

"Sorry," I said, "it won't fit in a hornbill."

During the night, I heard Mangualo singing with the other men through the rain, and for a delirious minute I thought they were chanting English words. *"Why on earth do we bother?"* It was starry and hot, the humidity breaking on the skin in cold drops, cicadas shrieking like referee whistles in the groves of rattan. Inside the tent, everything had begun to disintegrate; it was like the hovel of a hobo living in an underground tunnel. Our paranoia about mosquitoes meant that you had to unzip the door in a flash, dive in headfirst, and then zip it back shut in under a second. From the outside, it was funny to watch, the whole tent shaking and cursing. By eight, the candle was out and there was only the Kombai song wafting across the forest. But then you might have to get up and shit in the jungle, a terrifying ordeal—the buffoon naked in the rain, a camping light strapped to his forehead, enflamed from head to foot with skin rashes caused by deet, holding a soaking toilet roll, tiptoeing among the lethally poisonous spiders. As soon as you turned off the light for the sake of insectal anonymity, a hundred fireflies would descend on your head like flares, lighting you up for the benefit of the animal kingdom: Hey, look, boys, a human shitter for dinner! Stretched on my length of bark, I tried to write with wet pencils, suffocating under the rain fly. My hearing was now so acute that I had trouble concentrating on the inner voice that writes. The jungle produced a monumental noise—whistlings, cawings, shrill peeps, parrot calls. I was now covered with small wounds, thorn punctures, heat and chemical rashes, the skin unwashed in days, the hair growing at a quickened pace so that it was close to being Jesus-like. My nails were black, the tips of the fingers lacerated from clutching at trees coated with spikes. The worst threat was eye infections. I had some drops from Bangkok, which I used every day regardless. But mental cohesion, as I began to discover, is rooted in the respectability and cleanliness of the body. As your body goes to pot, so bit by bit does your mind. It is as if pieces of your internal structure begin falling away like chunks of plaster from a cheap statue. At the edges of this unraveling mental structure lies the shimmering hysteria to which I have alluded. Strangely, however, I was attracted to it. For when do you ever feel the power of encroaching hysteria? It is something buried in oneself that rarely rises to the surface. It is just pure disintegration in the end. But *after* your mind has disintegrated, what is left? Perhaps what you see in the eyes of a Kombai. But for them, perhaps the *kakua* were the symbols of this same disintegration.

At the beginning of his book on Papua, Tobias Schneebaum gives us a quote from Carleton Gajdusek's Papua New Guinea Journal for 1961. Gajdusek, one of America's most famous Renaissance man scientists, did critical work on prions and Creutzfeldt-Jakob disease among the Fore people in Papua New Guinea in the 1950s and had a long love affair with this magical island. One could say that the affair was literal—he had a pronounced taste for Papuan boys, whom he imported to his mansion in Maryland for years on "scholarships." Convicted by the FBI of child abuse, he fled to France, claiming to be the victim of a witch hunt. In any case, in his journal, which the FBI had confiscated, he wrote:

It is strange how mediocre all in civilization seems— art, journalism, philosophy, motion pictures and even music, whenever I leave or "come out from" the Papua New Guinea bush. I would have suspected the reverse . . . Perhaps it is their remoteness from the real nature of man and his natural world environment that makes them appear flat and unreal.

This was the other side of the disintegrative pain.

On the trail the next day a boy appeared out of nowhere, walking from tree house to tree house, a speared bird in his hand. His hair was threaded with pieces of wild orchid: wild sweetness in motion. He was also headed to our next tree house. It was a lucky break, for he had been at the pig feast the other day and remembered us. We wouldn't have to have the usual psychodrama upon our arrival.

The chief was called Mambi. He shook our hands with a papery warmth. *Nari nari nari.* The Kombai also now called me *nare*, "older brother." There was something moving about his tone. "We hope," he said—I thought wistfully, if a forest man can feel wistful—"that you'll come back one day to see us." It was the first time that a Kombai had expressed a desire to see us again.

We smoked in the early evening, flying foxes shrilling in the trees. At this point, I could not resist asking Mambi a question that had been nagging at me for some time. You see the missionary airplane going overhead, I asked him, but what do you think it is? You've seen it several times, no? But do you never wonder how or why it flies?

His head dangled listlessly and he bit his lower lip. "I just run away and hide when it passes overhead." The others all shook their heads and said the same.

So I explained that it was we white people who made the planes and made them fly. It was our machine, our way of getting about.

"So," Mambi asked unexpectedly, "how does it fly, then?"

I was halfway through my explanation of the dynamics of winged flight when I realized that I had no idea how airplanes fly. He looked intently at me, curious to see a man who could not explain how his own artifacts actually worked. And suddenly I dreaded his asking me how my flashlight worked or how my Gore-Tex boots were waterproof. About these marvelous inventions of my own culture I was essentially as ignorant as he—that is, he knew much more about his stuff than I knew about mine.

The next morning we went down to a claustrophobic part of the river closed in with massive sagos, men and women together. The men were going to cut down a sago tree with their hulking stone axes. The felling took an hour, hard and sweaty work. After the palm had come down, it was split open, and the women moved in with stone clubs to smash the interior to pulp. The pulp was then drained through a frond and rolled into balls. The men all sat down to smoke, and a soporific mood descended upon us. It was then that I looked up and saw Juha standing to one side in the forest surrounded by a large group of the younger boys. The tall Viking blond covered in butterflies, the boys shouting and stamping their feet. *Juha! Juha!* Construe this as one may, I couldn't help noticing how easy it was for humans apparently divided by immense differences to bond without language.

Later, we went for a swim.

There was a sinisterly opulent river below Mambi's tree house, its white sand beach sheltered by Pará rubber trees. A threat of crocodiles, and the water deep, opaquely cold. Malinowski's nirvana. We swam naked through interconnecting pools. There was now a sort of jungle-military comradeship between us, a nonverbal understanding of sorts. We had become a bit like the band of boys in *Lord of the Flies*, without, of course, the animosities or the need to kill pigs.

"I wonder," I said, "if the Kombai will stay the same after we leave. What will they be saying about us—what do they *think* about us?"

How does a forest people see whites, the product of millennia of innovation and striving? In Graham Greene's *A Burnt-Out Case*, mystified Africans sing about them: "Here is a white man who is neither a father nor a doctor. He has no beard. He comes from a long way away—we do not know from where—and he tells no one to what place he is going nor why. He is a rich man, for he drinks whisky every evening and he smokes all the time. Yet he offers no man a cigarette."

High up in the sky, trails of smoke appeared, drifting from the tree house. The cane grass was tall enough to cover a man, but it shivered and shook. The Lost Horizon or Shangri-La might be places consisting of this simple handful of elements: grass, water, light. In the far future, when the earth is a continuous tourist development connected by magnetic trains, there will be a fantasy based on these elements, for in effect there already is. The idyll of depopulated splendor has receded outward from the Lake District circa 1800 to Papua New Guinea in 2005. Whatever we may think about the grander economic forces of history, it is tourism that has effected this insane revolution, one that has pushed the romantic loner ever outward toward more violent ruptures with his own world. In the future, these environments will probably have to be carved out of game parks and patrolled reserves, like the pueblo of Malpais visited by the Alphas in *Brave New World*. The Kombai would be like the

Indian guides in Huxley's novel, their bodies painted, their "black hair braided with fox fur and red flannel," and their shoulders draped with turkey-feather capes. The Primitives who live outside the charmed world that is both brave and new. But it will, if possible, be much easier to visit them by helicopter.

From then on, the trails began to loop slowly back to Wanggemalo. On the GPS device, the "no data" zones alternated with foggy patches of digital terrain. We all began to get diarrhea. At one tree house there was an immense clearing overlaid by a lattice of interlocking logs. Below it, at the bottom of a steep hill, the river curled around islands of mud, and in the windless humidity here I began to get cold chills, as if a fever were breeding inside me. The men from the tree house came down at twilight and danced with us, holding hands and snapping their legs open at the knees like rubbery epileptics. We pranced about like this for an hour. A plate of bird eyes was produced. The men said, "To our surprise, you are not cold." Our dicks were wrapped in banana leaves and we smoked naked in the tree house, swaying like birds perched in a nest. Where are we? I thought, gazing out at mile upon mile of tossing palms.

"All night," the men said, "we have been talking about you." *But who were they?* I ate the eyes, in a state far beyond disgust.

"I am coming unstuck," I found myself saying to Juha. "Or something like that. Do you want to get back?"

"Yes and no. Yes." He grinned with reluctance. The enlightened man's reluctance.

"Perhaps. But then what did we come for?"

We came for a bit of heart of darkness, no? And yet the Kombai were rather sweet in the end. The heart of darkness wasn't them. It was Nature.

"But Nature here is what it *really* is. And now we're scared, no?"

When I looked out over the forest, I didn't feel fear. It was nothingness. A green ocean with no features, no past, no memory. I could see why the Kombai believed two things: that it was all there was in the world and that it was filled with *kakua-kumu*. This mass of seething Nature had form and shape, symbolic zest. Otherwise it would not have struck fear into them.

I began to dream about the trail itself. In my dreams it formed a series of endless loops going nowhere. But my own panic was not necessarily shared by the companions. For one thing, I was very mystified by how much better disciplined Georg and Theresia were, for every predawn I was woken by a Teutonically energetic zipping and unzipping of tent apertures as they neatly folded every article of their gear and stowed it into their waterproof bags, already ready to go an hour before the Milo came to the camp table. So our characteristics persist, even national ones. Juha went off on long, lonely meditations with his walking stick, looking exactly like the young Max von Sydow. Woolford and I, the Anglos, read our books and talked about the 2004 election, which had been decided in our absence. The Papuans loved saying the word "Bush." What could that sound mean?

The last hike was the hardest. At the far side of the sago swamps, slowed by heat exhaustion and diarrhea, I finally heard a cock crowing. It might as well have been Big Ben.

Some boys came running out into the jungle with armfuls of seersack fruit, whose flesh smells like Turkish delight and whose seeds are larger than olives. The villagers came to their doors to stare. We were soaked with mud, with haunted eyes and long beards now spattered with coconut fiber and seersack pips. So, they might have asked, how was your vacation? How was it being out of the world?

The women returned with the flying foxes and brush turkey eggs, which, when cooked, turned out to contain perfectly defined fetuses with eyes. The electrical storms raged through the evening, through our long, recuperative sleeps on the bunk beds and, in my case, on the porch, where I liked to slumber close to the rain. Brimob reappeared with some sweet potatoes for cooking and asked us with great politeness whom we had met and where. I had ferocious nightmares, in which the Kombai took a keen interest. The boys asked me questions. "How, Lorry, do you kill the *kakua* in *your* forest?"

I tried to describe New York. They shook their heads and spat.

I said I lived on an island in a tree house with forty-six women, none of whom I knew. I rarely went hunting these days. I sat by my fire eating frozen sago grubs, drinking fermented pond water, and watching out for demons. I sometimes went walking.

"Walking?"

Traveling, wandering. Just for fun.

"Shooting birds?"

"Sometimes."

"*Uey!* Shooting birds is fucking great."

But what was with the wandering for fun? Only *kakua* did that.

I opened the piano and tried to play. The Kombai collected their pay—paper money, though there was little use for it—and camped all over the house watching us. A harmonious chord coming out of the piano stilled them at once; they cocked their ears. In return they showed me how to clean the wax out of my ears with a sago grub. In the dusty glass of the house's one remaining window I could see how much thinner I was, and in light of the regime of Chiva-Som it was ironic to consider that I had now lost some twenty pounds.

When we left Wanggemalo, I gave my baseball cap to Boogie-Woogie Baby and my punctured Therm-a-Rest to Stephanus, who had hauled my pack through fifty miles of jungle and who would relish this rubber article as an objet d'art rather than as a deficient sleeping aid. There were sad leave-takings. It was Wanggemalo that now seemed like Manhattan, a veritable metropolis. The whole population came onto the airstrip to see us off, waving with a melancholy knowledge that we would never come back, though they said the very act of coming back would mean a great deal to them. Even the witch was there, waving with the others. The porters came and held on to our hands as they murmured our names, and the sound of the plane was intensely strange as it came back to us. I almost wanted to run into the bush and hide from it, as the core Kombai did. Tears in the eyes: who would have expected it? And the plaintive,

"Come back, Lorry, come back and see us!" I could imagine the party that would erupt if I ever did.

After a night in Wamena, cold in the rain, we flew back to the coast—to Jayapura, to Sentani, to the Javans with their pale skins and their abundance of motorbikes, to the world of cold Cokes and pillows. There was a ritual shaving of the beards and haircuts in a small Javan barbershop across the street. The equally ritual first Coke burned the mouth and the throat. The *coldness* of which civilization is capable is impressive. The hotel itself now felt like the Hilton, or a small, comfortable lunatic asylum. Just to have a bed, a washbasin, a bucket of cold water in a corner and a plastic scoop. At night, to see the candles lit on the betel tables all along the road and to see the headlights skimming along it. *The Life of Chopin* was still playing on the TV, and the Russians still came out for breakfast in their airline shirts and beach shorts. It rained day and night. I lay on the bed shivering, sleeping for hours, dreaming, chain-smoking. A beautiful young German girl appeared in the room next door, all dressed up in jungle gear—a young anthropologist about to go off to do fieldwork on the Yanimura River. She seemed nervous, spooked by the goofy vibe of a Papuan town. I heard her clicking away on her laptop all night. She wanted to hear stories about the Kombai. She said we all looked "wasted but healthy." How could I not think of the young Mead?

Unsurprisingly, the German girl had been inspired by Mead's one-woman expeditions to places off the maps of her time. She herself was writing a thesis about Papua, as so many Ph.D. anthropologists did these days. She was certainly an anomaly at the Blue Hotel. The Russians stared at her in lyrical astonishment. The Papuan staff had probably never seen a blond woman before, at least not an attractive one. She looked like Chopin's wife.

And so, by a delicious coincidence, my last hours on the island of New Guinea were spent talking about Mead with a woman called Melanie, whose white arms seemed extraordinary now, as tender as the arms of Mead in those early photographs from the late '20s and early '30s where she looks like a child—as she herself famously complained. But in fact it was the later Mead that concerned me now, the aging woman who returned to the Sepik River in 1967 to see how modernity had played itself out in this backwater that in 1938 had been so poetically raw. She wrote that she was filled with apprehension. Had the tall, gabled houses of the Tambunam remained the same, with their supernatural faces woven into the façades? Did shamans still dance among the killed crocodiles? In many ways, it is the most interesting moment of the *Letters*, for it is the heartbreak of change that most acutely calls into doubt our experience of the world. We had been asking ourselves the same questions in the forest: will we change the Kombai by giving them a candle? The myth of tourism is constructed around places that purport not to change—Disneyland, for example, does not change much, nor does the average resort. Tourist environments are a way of pretending that death will not prevail after all. Their atmosphere is one of the eternal present; inside them, it is as if time has been brought to an ingenious standstill. But what happens when the tourist goes back to the same place thirty years later? Does he ever feel *better* about the place? Does it ever seem that the place has improved? Not likely.

The tourist culture (a good way of describing our culture in general) has ceased to think about aging, or how it is to be done with elegance and dignity, and it has done this because it has ceased to think much about experience at all. The whole premise of the tourist economy, after all, is that experience can be bought for money. That it can be commodified. The powerful interactions of adults have even disappeared almost entirely from the surface of the culture at large. Do you have to go to Papua to refind them? The bonds forged with this small band of fellow mammalian humans on this antitouristic "touristic" venture were atavistically vivid: they struck me as very nineteenth century, just as Mead's letters did, with their romantic excitements and human curiosity.

This is, in fact, how Mead experienced her return to the Papuan paradise of the Tambunam, where the gabled houses still stood tall but where the "men's things" had been burned in a bombing raid during the Second World War, where the old gods had been banished by Christianity, and where head-hunting had been replaced by commercial carving for tourists:

On this return to Tambunam it has become very clear to me that it is only through this kind of intense living in face-to-face relationships that the life and culture of a whole people can be fully experienced. It is through the records of such closely bound lives that we may hope to understand the human need for continuity, repetitive experience and intimacy. For intimacy has its sources in just these familiar repetitions of laughter at old jokes, remembered anger at old quarrels, meals

eaten together in the same twilight and children listen-
ing to accounts of things that happened before their
parents were born, stories told and re-told. And here
in Tambunam, where change is still in the making,
repetition binds the present to the past and to the future; repetition binds the events all of us recall to the
events that now will be recorded.

POSTSCRIPT: WHEREVER

Throughout this journey I had had the same feeling that I had not been "abroad" anywhere, that I had simply moved through different dimensions of a single human contemporaneity. For months afterward, in the middle of a New York winter I would find myself sleepwalking through my apartment saying, *"Umbiago!"* and sitting in a corner of the front room waiting for a Kombai story to begin. One needs to be exorcised after a long voyage, but we no longer have priests or shamans we can believe in.

In his travelogue about France, *In the White Cities*, Joseph Roth writes:

> Ever since I've been in hostile countries, I no longer feel foreign in any of them. I never go "abroad" any more. That's a leftover from the days of the stagecoach! At most I might go somewhere "new." And there I see that I had already intuited it. But I can't "report" on it. At the most I can say how the experience felt, to me.

So it is. But a year later I was driving along the Kona coast of Hawaii's Big Island, and as I wandered around

Hawaii's surreally vacuous landscape—a kind of New Jersey tropical-style—I couldn't help wondering if this was how Papua New Guinea would end up in the imaginable near future. Hawaii had been depopulated of natives, turned into a large sugar plantation, and finally acquired by the United States through a farcically engineered coup in 1893. Formal annexation came in 1900 with the wonderfully named Organic Act.

The monoculture of sugar had paved the way for the monoculture of tourism. For once monoculture has become second nature to a landscape, this exchange can happen easily. Sugar or tourism, it is the same principle.

The southern Kona coast is richly volcanic, dominated by the coffee farms that succeeded the sugar plantations. The road is congested with tourist traffic. Coffee shops packed with pensioner tour buses, retirement homes, beach parks: every inch is saturated. Halfway up the coast stands the island's principal archaeological site, the Pu`uhonua O Honaunau National Historical Park, and a short way beyond it Captain Cook, a place split in two by the roaring highway. To one side of the road stands the coffee-colored 1929 Manago Hotel, one of many dusty relics of Hawaii's Japanese immigrant past. There's a Señor Billy's Cantina drive-thru Mexican and a corroded tin shack marked with the words "Art Farm." The Kona Theater has long been boarded up. Below lies the blue bay where Cook met his grisly end, murdered by the Hawaiians after a misunderstanding. He had appeared out of the blue in January of the year 1779, a dead ringer for the god Lono. All went well until his ship departed on February 4, only to return a week later after being battered by a storm. It seemed like an evil omen to the Hawaiians, and their erstwhile hospitality turned to ire. No one seems to know exactly what happened. There was an altercation on the beach and four Englishmen died. Captain Cook found his immortality; centuries later, his blunders are taken as symptomatic of the European penetration of the virginal tropics.

There was a similarity between the monstrous planned resorts and sugar plantations. Both were self-sufficient in their way, carving the landscape up to their uses, designed as enclaves against an unknown hinterland. And of all the Kona resorts, none is as plantationlike as the Hilton Waikoloa Village, built along a stretch of coast called South Kohala and called, of course, "Disneyland" by locals. When it opened in 1988 at a cost of $360 million, it called itself the most expensive resort ever built. One could hardly ask for a more perfect expression of the spirit of monoculture. I went in for tea and then, on a whim, checked in.

Built over sixty-two acres, the Hilton sports a car park whose dimensions are clearly designed to awe and confuse. Inside, the lobby is served by a monorail that courses through the resort like a commuter train in Singapore. I paused for a moment to check out that night's in-house entertainment: Desiree Cruz, Ginger Berlemenn, Terri Spruill in the Malolo Lounge. The crowd was a mix of ancient American and juvenile Japanese. A lady whom I thought I recognized said, in a loud voice, *"Mais c'est très Hong Kong!"* Below me was a canal bordered by enormous Chinese vases and fragments of pseudo-Buddhist-temple architecture. A launch roared past on it with a Just Married sign. Aimlessly, I took the monorail to a thing called the Boat Landing Pavilion. We passed by an artificial beach, snaking

lagoons filled with small sharks and exotic fish, Buddha statues, Chinese lions, coffee-colored concrete towers, endless
potted palms. Yellow kayaks zoomed by on the canal. A guy
in white naval uniform served as conductor. Around me,
grim-faced Japanese couples stared blankly at it all, perhaps
stunned by the down-at-the-heels feel of the place, for there
is no question that these days Asia has resorts and hotels far
superior to anything that the United States can offer, and at
a fraction of the price.

In the lobby, I wandered for a while down a one-mile-
long gallery extending on either side of it and filled with art
exhibits from all over Polynesia. And thus I came to a large
collection of material from Papua New Guinea. There was a
partial reconstruction of a Papuan house, masks, arrows,
implements, magical artifacts, sago skirts. Not far away
there was a show of Samoan stuff. Families stopped in front
of them for a few seconds, sniffed, and moved on, humming
to themselves. The cornucopia of the South Seas, which have
given us the desert island, Robinson Crusoe, Margaret Mead
and modern anthropology, Bali Hai, the noble savage, and
the decors of Club Med—not to mention the Hilton
Waikoloa itself. The sad tropics in all their flattened diver-
sity.

Thereafter I retreated to my room, which enjoyed a view
over the artificial beach and the artificial lagoon. I closed the
curtains, ordered some room service sushi, and turned on
the TV for a few days. I couldn't say why watching TV was
so soothing now, so appropriate. I had, in any case, an infal-
lible sense that that was what everyone else was doing. From
time to time I peeked through the resort curtains and
watched the fellow inmates boarding a launch with its uni-

formed conductor. How long can you spend in such a place without being noticed? At night I went down to the outdoor café and had a plate of teriyaki shrimp, then boarded a launch bound for the Malolo Lounge, where I could order a gin and tonic with a paper umbrella and watch Terri Spruill go through her set. It was uproarious. I whistled as I applauded. Desiree Cruz was even better. In a way, I was quite happy. Before long, I thought, I would probably start forgetting everything that had happened. A few days would go by, then a few weeks. I would get a tan on the artificial beach and, if all went well, I might meet a horny widow from Michigan or, better still, Osaka. I would get a personal trainer in the meantime and work out every morning, and perhaps every evening too, in the Aloha Fitness Center, if that was what it was called. If I got bored, I could read Lévi-Strauss; if I got homesick for the South Seas, I could go to the gallery of exhibits.

The sun shone every day in exactly the same way, the palms waving in a symmetrical line against the blue of the sea. I explored my little world thoroughly, just as Crusoe had done. I learned a lot about Hawaiian culture. Before long I was something of a connoisseur in the nuances of the indigenous Kona coffee, which was available in all the cafés. However, it never occurred to me that I might want to meet a Hawaiian, for where would one meet a Hawaiian in Hawaii? Such questions belong to another age. And as you are working out in the gym they even seem distinctly quaint, if not impertinent. But what of the people I had met on my Gulliverian travels? Before long, sad to say, I could no longer remember the faces of Hamza Mustafa, Manish Chakraborti, Dr. Jeff my nutritionist at Chiva-Som, or even the flamboyant Chief Yali. It was all flattened inside my memory, where it belonged, where one's travels always end up. The traveler always forgets his travels.

However, one has to keep on traveling. The next year, I firmly resolved, I would go to Madagascar, because I had never been to Madagascar, not even once, and everyone these days went to Madagascar. There was even a Hilton there, overlooking a thing called Lake Anosy. Next year, I thought to myself at the end of each day as the ukulele music wafted up from the bandstand on the lagoon, next year, in any case, I'll be somewhere else.